The Forgiveness

What Your Therapist Isn't Going to Tell You

EDWIN L ANDERSEN

with

THOMAS M SHENK

WISDOMGUIDES© PUBLICATIONS
Pasadena, California

The Truth About Forgiveness
What Your Therapist Isn't Going to Tell You

Copyright © 2018 Edwin L Andersen

Self-Help > Spirituality > Personal Development

ISBN–13: 978-0-692-05361-4

All rights reserved. No part of this publication may be reproduced, stored in a retrieval system or transmitted in any form or by any means, electronic, mechanical, photocopying, recording or otherwise, without prior permission of the publisher.

Biblical references are from the New Revised Standard Version (NRSV), unless otherwise noted. Copyright © 1991, 1994 by Oxford University Press, Inc. Content from *Lessons of the Wild, Learning from the Wisdom of Nature*, Copyright © 2009 by Edwin L Andersen, used with permission from the author.

FIRST EDITION

01 02 03 04 05 06 07 08 09 10

WisdomGuides© Publications
Pasadena, California
www.wisdomguides.org

Cover Design Edwin L Andersen
Front cover photograph in the public domain
FreePhotos,HQ101.com
Rear cover photograph by Bill Youngblood

V8.0.9 01 SC2018 20190118

TO

Everyone who showed us
the way to forgiven-ness

Contents

    Introduction

1 Life is Hard   1

2 Hole in the Soul   29

3 The Enemy is Us   53

4 Messenger in Blue   71

5 Feeding of Wolves   91

6 The Greatest Secret   105

7 Your Brother's Keeper   129

8 Getting There from Here   149

    Epilogue   177

    Keys to Forgiveness   189

    Vocabulary   191

    Wisdom Books   192

    Making a Grateful Box   193

    Bibliography   194

INTRODUCTION

Not long ago, I opened my inbox and found this message:

> We are human, fragile and frail creatures all with plenty of fault and imperfections and weaknesses. All of us. Recognizing them is not easy sometimes. Usually it occurs by stepping outside of oneself and looking in and sometimes it takes events like this. I greatly appreciate your note! No more need be said. A hug, a handshake, no more discussion of such. It's over. Stay healthy.

The man who sent the message and I had a falling out over something I said and did which grievously offended him. When we parted company, there was more than a little "unfinished business" between us. Many months passed without any communication, until he emailed me "an olive branch." I was still regretful and conflicted by my role in the breakup, so I took time to think things over before I responded. I found myself at the inescapable nexus point of choice; having to choose between reconciliation and the certain dissolution of a forty-year relationship. The irony of rejecting another man's peace offering, while at the same time writing a book on forgiveness, seemed highly duplicitous to me. So, I responded affirmatively by taking full responsibility for my inappropriate actions and as humbly as I could asked for my friend's forgiveness. His immediate and unqualified acceptance stirred my deepest emotions and I joyfully emerged from my "inner drama of the soul," relieved that we had renewed our long friendship.

This book is written for anyone who is suffering through their own inner drama of the soul. As my friend noted in his email, we are frail, faulty creatures, doomed to experience pain and humiliation as we walk the trail of life. *Suffering is inevitable, and sadly enough, we seem to bring much of it on ourselves.* None of us has the power to regulate everything that happens to us, but we do have full autonomy in making our response. We can choose to hold on to our pain, or we can learn the art of letting go.

The Truth About Forgiveness is a collaborative effort by two men who have spent the last several decades encouraging people to embrace suffering as an essential feature of the human condition. In this vocation, we have been blessed to interact with folks from many stations of life, at every point along the way. We are fortunate to have made deep and lasting connections among the men and women with whom we have worked. Writer Frederick Buechner posits, "The kind of work God usually calls you to is the kind of work (a) that you need most to do and (b) that the world most needs to have done. *The place God calls you to is the place where your deep gladness and the world's deep hunger meet.*"[1] People are both our business and our calling, and we wouldn't have it any other way.

Over the years, we have developed a practical orthodoxy that is affirmed again and again by the people we meet. Following are a few of the foundational beliefs and observations that animate our vision to leave the world better than the one in which we live. All people need to feel that they are a "good person," that they are making a positive contribution to someone else's welfare. Even those who act badly believe there is some good to be achieved by their behavior. While we have seen our share of unhappy people, we have never known a person who sincerely

---

[1] Frederick Buechner, *Wishful Thinking, A Seeker's ABC* (New York: Harper One, 1993), 118–19. Emphasis mine.

wishes to stay that way. *The desire for happiness is deeply embedded in our DNA, yet it has become tragically elusive for people living in these post-modern times.* We are convinced that there really *is* such a thing as a "mid-life crisis." Not everyone is willing to investigate the nagging feeling of wanting to do more in the second half of their life, but great treasures await those who make the journey inward. We have found a direct correlation between experiencing the inner life and finding happiness as we grow older. One of Tom's favorite maxims is, "*Every truly happy person I meet who is over fifty is on a spiritual journey!*" This inner life is lived at our deepest level of consciousness, in the dimension of our souls. We subscribe to the idea of God, the Ultimate Reality, who is both a mystery and an indubitable part of life's experience. The daily practice of prayer and contemplation, done in pure quietude, can lead us into a profound relationship with our Creator, a relationship that cannot otherwise be established.

We are skeptics of both randomness and strict determinism as explanations for the things that happen. Its elegant rhythms convince us that life happens for reasons, often reasons we do not, or cannot understand. The element of chance has for us been transformed into a sublime pattern of "holy coincidences." Each and every one of us is an integral part of the great web of life, endowed with a purpose and a destiny. Living presents us with an endless series of decision-making moments, where we have the power to choose which road we will take.

In our journey together we will discuss a model for forgiveness that has proven to effectively remedy the hurts that people feel when they are out of sync with the rest of the world. We all screw up, and sooner or later we are bound to do something that injures another human being. Forgiveness is the antidote for diseases of the heart like enmity, bitterness, fear, resentment and regret that result from ours' or another person's actions. This book was written to help people repair their fractured relationships and find the place of lasting peace. "Letting go" is the term we use for freeing oneself from the demons that haunt us on our pilgrimage through life. People begin to let go when they decide that the pain of holding on to their hurt is no longer worth it. Our goal is that readers will find hope in the words we have written and the stories we have told.

As you are about to discover, there is probably nothing entirely original in the book. Tom and I have been enriched by the wisdom and generosity of those who have already found the way and left their markers along the trail. We make no apology for taking writer's license in liberally sharing quotes and stories from these inimitable trailblazers. In the final analysis, we admit that we don't know all that much, save what a man gleans from seven decades of living.

We formed *WisdomGuides.org* a few years ago as our "skin in the game," to ensure that we are being true to our values. This initiative has given us a way to explore what it really means to be men and seek out the highest purpose for our lives. We stake no special claim on wisdom, praying only that we will have good companions as we walk through the wilderness toward the light of truth. Frankly, we have been surprised—sometimes overwhelmed—by what we have been taught by the young men in our Cadre Adventures.

Most of the credit for these pages surely belongs to all the beautiful people who trustingly shared their stories in a thousand fragile, tender moments. Their candor and openness to vulnerability allowed us to fathom the depths of the human heart to a level that made *The Truth About Forgiveness* possible. Without their willing participation there would not be much of a tale to tell or a book to write.

Your approach to this book

Except for the quotations, Ed Andersen wrote most the text and collated the material for *The Truth About Forgiveness*. Tom Shenk was there every step of the way, not only contributing the behavioral aspects of the book, but many anecdotes and stories, as well.

We have crafted the book to read like a travelogue, a wisdom journey into the interior of your heart and soul. We know there are concepts and ideas herein that are challenging, even threatening for some. Our purpose is to encourage you to get out of your comfort zone and examine your motives and actions in relation to the world around you.

We rely heavily on storytelling to get our points across. Most of the stories are based on true events, while the rest are plausible scenarios that often happen in real life. We ask many questions throughout, which we hope will evoke—perhaps provoke—a written response from you. We challenge you to take advantage of these opportunities to test your beliefs and motivations. Each of us has our particular biases and perspectives. While ours should become evident to you, consider your own in light of what you read in the pages ahead.

It might have been justly named "The Big Why Bother Book." Why bother writing this book, when some of the stories will seem trite and corny? Please remember this: When forgiveness of any kind is appropriate, and we do not act, we are choosing to live with anxiety; and that is not a "healthy" decision. We bother because we care!

Please know in advance that, while we use "God language," our goal is not to convert anyone to anything, lest it be the power of forgiveness. We respect the idea that each individual comes to spirituality from their own vector of experience, so God (your Higher Power) may be whomever you have found him or her to be. We encourage you to navigate your way to the final page, even if you are uncomfortable with some of the concepts we present. Your openness to a "new see" in your life will be beneficial the next time you find yourself in distress.

Second only to "I love you," the most powerful words in any language are, "I am sorry!" What would the world be like if everyone learned to use these words more often?

□

⚷ Keys denote ideas central to a deeper understanding of forgiveness. These ideas call for a personal response from the reader. They are listed on page 189.

V "V" in the margin indicates a term that is defined or described in detail in the *WisdomGuides*© *Vocabulary* on page 191.

1

LIFE IS HARD

"Smooth seas do not make a skillful sailor."
AFRICAN PROVERB

I was five years old when the perfect world I knew came to a sudden end. I awakened from a dreamy sleep to hear the familiar voices of two angry people, who were just beyond my bedroom door. I still vividly recall the terrifying loneliness that drove me down, deep into my bed covers, sobbing and wondering why my mother and father were saying such mean things to each other. The reason for their argument centered on something my father had done—something that must have been very bad. Such encounters became commonplace, and I learned that Dad had a problem with the stuff that came in the fancy square bottle stored high up in the pantry. I began to see that his problem was causing them to drift apart, but I could not have known then that my parents' hostilities toward one another would have negative emotional and psychological effects on me later. Dad's struggle with alcohol persisted for another thirty years, until Mom finally filed for divorce, which so unsettled my father that he stopped drinking. By then, I had moved out and made a life of my own, but the scars of those early years stayed with me for a very long time. Though he stubbornly remained sober for the rest of his life, the pain that my father caused the family and me was something that didn't go away easily.

I came to the realization that my mother, despite her nurturing heart, was also responsible for much of the anguish I experienced as a boy. During their time together, Mom took a lot of abuse from my father, but she waited too long to summon the courage to leave him. She had many of her own personal issues, not surprisingly stemming from a very difficult childhood. When Mom was only two, her mother suddenly died. During the lean times leading up to the Great Depression, a motherless toddler was a major liability on a mid-western farm, so she was sent away to live with a woman in town. Some years later, her older brother brought her back to live with the family, but by then the damage had already been done. Though we seldom spoke about it, I am certain my mother had deep regrets about how this chapter of her life played out, how she was exiled from those closest to her and forced to live with someone whom she didn't really care for very much. As time went on, Mom's spirit broke. She gave us the best years of her life, but was deprived of much happiness because of the dysfunction in our home. Although she dutifully persevered in an unhappy marriage for the benefit of my siblings and me, in retrospect I think it was a mistake.

When I look back on my teen years, I confess that I was an accomplice to my father's addiction. I loved to bowl and often spent my earnings as a paper boy at the local bowling alley. One afternoon, ostensibly for a father and son outing, Dad took me to the iconic Surf Bowl down by the pier. I was on top of my game that day, and after applauding my efforts for a time, Dad made his way into the bar. I was faced with a dilemma. I really wanted to continue "strutting my stuff," but I knew where Dad's drinking would lead. My ego prevailed and I selfishly bowled several more games, but not before my father's condition had deteriorated into drunkenness. I was only fourteen, so Dad had to drive us home. I regret that I didn't show more strength by confronting him and insisting that we leave before things got out of hand.

I don't want to paint a gloomy picture of my childhood, for all things considered I had a charmed upbringing. I remain deeply indebted to my mother and my father for giving me as much love as they could and for providing me with both the means and opportunity to have a successful life. However, the peace that I know now in this, the best time of my life, derives much from an understanding of the sources of my anger and the awareness that I still bear the scars of my parents' mistakes.

Kindred spirits

You too may have been raised in an environment where things were not right, where your mother or father made choices that hurt you. You might have experienced the deterioration of your family circle because of the actions of an irresponsible parent or relative. Perhaps you lost the intimate bond you once had with a brother or sister or another person dear to you. These conditions may not be relegated to your past; you could be living in difficult circumstances at this very moment. If my story sounds all too familiar, I am sorry—sorry that you have had to endure such hurtful things. Sadly, you are not alone. There are millions of us who carry these same deep scars. Have you ever wondered how someone can fall from grace so precipitously and so tragically? Clearly, the stresses and strains of life often bring out the worst in people. We live in an achievement oriented society that puts relentless pressure on people to succeed. Success usually means earning a substantial living, getting ahead of the next guy and maintaining an enviable lifestyle. Having to compete and the resulting temptation to compare yourself to others can be hard on a person.

The withering pace of contemporary living takes its toll on just about everyone, especially those who have personal and financial obligations beyond themselves. Many men and women with children are not equipped to handle the enormous responsibilities that come with being a parent. Given what we know, it shouldn't surprise us when we see people lose their ability to cope with life's demands.

Many seek escape in all the wrong places, hoping to deaden their pain in deleterious ways: drug and alcohol abuse, sexual promiscuity, pornography, habitual gambling, just to name a few. Given enough time, these harmful practices lead us down the wrong path and inevitably diminish who we are. I saw this happen to someone who was once very close to me.

David had his share of difficulties in growing up. He was the proverbial middle child, and as such, received none of the affirmation of the family's first-born. Nor did he get nearly the attention lavished on his younger sister. His interests were outside of school and it was evident that David was not destined to match his older brother's success in the classroom. In 1963, the two boys gained admission to a prestigious prep school, and while his brother easily handled the transition, David struggled and was forced to return home, an academic failure. "Why can't you be like your big brother?" was a resounding message that was drummed into him in a thousand subtle, and some not so subtle, ways. David was a shy, quiet person, who kept a lot of his frustrations and anger bottled up inside. He was likeable, but he had a temper and could erupt like a volcano, so those who knew him were careful not to say or do things that might set him off. David turned his attention to individual pursuits where he could build self-esteem, earn the respect of his peers and gain acceptance from his father. He loved physical challenges and he became a trophy winning wrestler. He was introduced to the martial arts, swiftly ascending to one of the highest levels of black belt in judo. David proved good with his hands and had instinctive skills as an automotive mechanic. When he was just sixteen he hitchhiked north to work for a mining operation in the wilds of Alaska. The ten-day trek through Canada on the ALCAN Highway cost him less than twenty dollars, most of which was spent on a cheap rain jacket.

In his twenties, he established a partnership with a friend in a classic car restoration business. Some of the finest antique automobiles in the country showed up in their shop. David purchased and refurbished a number of his own vintage autos, which earned prestigious awards at the premier car shows. Meanwhile, he continued to work as a machine specialist and production manager for a local produce packing company.

Sometime in the mid 1970's, David signed up for a college extension course in Native American basketry. This took him to the Klamath River region of California, where he was introduced to renowned basket weavers from the Hupa, Yurok and Karok tribes. He was soon accepted by these women and even lived among them for a time. He eventually earned the trust of tribal leaders and received the rarest of invitations when asked if he wished to become a full-fledged member of the tribe. Although he declined, he still participated in the ritual life of the tribe and became known as a man possessing considerable spiritual powers. David mastered the art of basket weaving to such a degree that when he brought examples of his work to the Phoebe Hearst Museum at the University of California at Berkeley in 2000, the curator remarked that his baskets were "as good as the ones we have in our display cases."

David reached many high points along the way, but he couldn't shake the shadows of his early life. He suffered heartbreak through two annulments, a long relationship that ended badly and a broken engagement that sent him into a tailspin. In David's case, the hope for a happy life that every good parent tries to give to their child never materialized. Despite his accomplishments and apparent success, the "hole in his soul" was never filled, and it seemed as if the life was just sucked out of him. He began using prescription drugs to kill the pain. He smoked marijuana to help him forget that he had failed to live up to the bright promise of his youth. David never forgave himself for being human and he refused to ask God, or anyone else, for their forgiveness and support. This man whom I once knew "died" fifteen years ago. Only the shell of a man named "David" is left, wandering hopelessly through the remainder of his life. He is the prisoner of his past, captive in the shackles of his unforgiven-ness.[1] He is the victim of anger and resentment, no longer the person he once was. This is one of the saddest stories I will ever tell. No one should end up this way. This is why we are writing this little book, hoping that you will learn the transformative power of forgiveness. Let us show you the trail to a happier life.

---

[1] For a description of unforgiven-ness, refer to footnote 2, page 31.

Forgiveness myths

In postmodern psychology and psychiatry, the secular mindset predominates. Contemporary psychoanalysis hinges, not on any ultimate truth or value, but on the idea that all reality is relative, grounded in culture through one's own history, language and experience. In what has become a rapidly growing clinical field, people with mental and emotional illnesses are "cured" through therapies constructed between doctor and patient. Philosopher Allan Bloom summed up developments in psychotherapy when he wrote: "The self is the modern substitute for the soul."[2]

Over the past few decades, the trend in philosophy has been to repudiate the traditional belief that humans have a singular identity, or soul. This view has been widely supplanted by the idea of many selves, which operate strictly in the social context in a two dimensional world of time and space.[3] For the secularist there is nothing beyond the physical world to require adherence to immutable principles or beg accountability to a higher authority. *WisdomGuides*© does not align itself with this materialistic school of thought.[4]

While not denying the efficacy of the modern secular approach in remedying much of the pain in our lives, there is a hitch. In renouncing permanence and a transcendent reality, we are free to create our own realities to fit our individual needs and purposes. We

---

[2] Alan Bloom, *The Closing of the American Mind* (New York: Simon & Schuster, 1988), 173.

[3] This idea is well expressed by Mitchell Stephens, *Los Angeles Times Magazine,* "To Thine Own Selves be True," https://www.nyu.edu/classes/stephens/Postmodern%20psych%20page.htm, (September 3, 2016).

[4] *WisdomGuides*© is an independent, not-for-profit group that works primarily with men to help them realize their gifts and talents as they seek the purpose for their lives. Visit *www.wisdomguides.org*.

thus become accountable only to ourselves and to other members of the society in which we live. The notion of "sin" is often denounced as part of a devious scheme by religious authorities to keep people under their control by preying on their fears and feelings of guilt.[5]

Secularists argue that, unlike people of faith, they use "reason and scientific principles" to reach their conclusions. Oddly enough, we believers also rely on our mental faculties and we arrive at very different conclusions about the nature of human beings and our place in the universe. We see serendipitous patterns underlying all of life and have been persuaded that something big is going on here, something much bigger than us! Our experience leads us to conclude that personal accountability goes beyond forgiving ourselves and making up with people we offend by promising to be better next time. The postmodern approach to forgiveness just doesn't go far enough; it evades the deeper implications of our wrong actions.

Prior to the last century, few credible thinkers would have denied the difference between the human brain and the mind. But in a matter of a few generations, this distinction has all but disappeared. Science, absent the capacity to quantify non-material entities like the mind, conveniently equates it with the brain. We take the contrarian's view, believing that the mind is a distinct entity that operates independently of the brain and transcends time and space. The mind is our portal to the eternal dimension, connecting us to the very Source of Life. Our mind is our direct link to the world of Spirit. Without a soul and the means to connect at a spiritual level of consciousness, life can have no ultimate meaning and destiny.

So what is the real story behind forgiveness? In this literary sojourn, we will attempt to explain why we see

---

[5] "Transcendent reality" refers to the spiritual dimension and infers the existence of a Supreme Being.

the world so differently from many of our contemporaries and why we think forgiveness begins and ends with God.

When We Hurt

Before we get into the meaning of forgiveness, we should first look at a human experience with which we are all too familiar—pain and suffering. This book deals, not so much with physical pain, but with the emotional kind and our response to it.

When we blame (point the finger at) someone else, this becomes our personal ticket to power, however short lived it might be. Blame allows us to assume a position of moral superiority and we often demonstrate this by being offended (taking something personally). Watch it happen in the world. How often do we observe someone who thinks and acts as if they are in some way better than someone else? How many times do we favorably compare ourselves to other people? Such judgements of others are intended to keep us from having to deal with our own unresolved issues. When our focus is outward we are looking to relieve our pain by having someone to hate or denigrate. This masks our inner shame and anxiety, providing us with a false sense of innocence. We want "peace" and we seek it by noticing the evil "over there." This of course is a temporary peace and is really no peace at all.[6]

Defining forgiveness

Perhaps the best way to adequately define forgiveness

---

[6] This section has been adapted from ideas presented by Richard Rohr, *"Transforming Our Pain,"* https://cac.org/transforming-our-pain-2016-07-03/, (January 2, 2018).

is to start with what forgiveness is *not*. Forgiveness is not letting the offender off the hook by offering flimsy, irrational excuses for someone's ill actions. This corrupted kind of compassion does not hold the offender accountable and sends the message that there are no consequences for hurting others. Just as in the case of a criminal offense, justice must be served. Those who verbally, physically or emotionally damage other persons must be held to account.

I am told that Mark Twain once quipped, "Denial ain't just a river in Egypt." Forgiveness is not trying to forget that you were hurt and dismissing bad behavior as if it never happened. This subversive form of denial never works in the long run. Continuing denial fosters a condition experts refer to as "self-loathing." When we become aware that we are hiding something hurtful that we haven't faced up to, we unconsciously grow to dislike ourselves. Self-loathing often morphs into hatred of entire groups of people, creating negative racial, ethnic and religious stereotypes. Self-awareness of this condition comes from deep reflection, where the truth about our feelings, perceptions and prejudices comes to the fore. People who loathe themselves cannot regain their emotional equilibrium alone. They will always require the help and support of a community of caring people.

We do not diminish the value of denial as a short term coping mechanism for dealing with our problems. There may be times in our lives, just like the proverbial camel that couldn't carry another straw on its back, when we just can't handle any more anxiety. These are the moments when we might have to suppress certain issues and deal with them at a later time. *However, the statute of limitations on our pain will eventually run out and then we are best advised to confront what happened.*

Forgiveness should never be a reflex reaction to bad things that happen to us. Indeed, anyone who forgives their transgressor too quickly might come to second guess themselves later. Consider the horrific events that took place on the evening of June 17, 2015 in Charleston, South Carolina. A 21-year old white man entered the First AME Church and took a seat in the pews among the all black congregation. According to eye witnesses, he sat and listened for a time, but then suddenly flew into a rage and began shouting racial epithets. He pulled a gun from his backpack and started shooting. Nine people, including the senior pastor, lost their lives that night. The perpetrator, after failing to end his life, was captured by law enforcement personnel and arrested for murder. What followed next is truly astonishing. Within days, several of the victims' family members came forward and, citing the Biblical mandate, offered their forgiveness to the murderer. Some even visited him in his jail cell and told him that they were praying for God to have mercy on his soul. Nevertheless, the man who assassinated nine of his fellow citizens showed no visible signs of remorse.[7]

The conditions of such a heinous act by an unrepentant perpetrator, followed so quickly by gestures of forgiveness on the part of the survivors, presents us with a perplexing picture. Understandably, the forgivers were looking for a way to deal with their tragic loss and some of them openly acknowledged their struggles with anger and revenge as they pondered their response. Privately, their Christian faith provided them with the solace they needed in trying to make sense of things and begin to move on. Publicly, the immediacy of their compassion for the killer was beneficial for a grieving community, but the process of individual healing will take much longer. It

---

[7] Jesse Holland, *The Associated Press,* "Forgiveness of Charleston Church Shooter Prompts Discussion," http://bigstory.ap.org/article/c0139482a 2724e2cba9e5f777f7af163/forgiveness-charleston-church-shooter-prompts-discussion, (July 4, 2015).

is usually best to consider its implications, so that when you do offer your forgiveness, it will bring you a lasting feeling of peace.

Though we see forgiveness and apology on the same continuum of human interaction, we find an important distinction. This distinction relates to the intent of the person who caused the problem. For instance, if you inadvertently bump into someone, good manners dictate that you make an apology by saying, "Excuse me," or "I'm sorry." Since it was clearly accidental, the other party will seldom be offended and will soon forget about it. However, if you are angry and deliberately shove another person, you violate the norms of good behavior, perhaps even the law. Now, a simple "I'm sorry" will be insufficient to make up for your bad behavior. The offended party deserves an explanation, showing that you are remorseful and willing to make amends. The words, "I'm sorry" have a different connotation in each these situations. The first says, "Sorry this happened. Hope you're OK." The second says, "I intentionally did something wrong to injure you and I am sorry. Please forgive me."

When we offer a sincere, heartfelt apology, our intent is not to "feel better" about ourselves. It is about getting in touch with the harm we have caused; it is about *being and doing better*. Remember, asking for forgiveness does not absolve us from being held accountable and is only the beginning of making full restitution. When genuine, an appeal for forgiveness begins the process of change in us, as well as in the person(s) we offended. The goal is to achieve a permanent shift in our behavior.

Convenient apology

Apologizing for an offense is sometimes just a cursory admission of error, rather than a confession of true contrition. Consider the litany of notable public figures shown on camera saying and doing some pretty bad things. Once they are called to account, here is what these offenders typically say: "I am truly sorry that this happened, I should have used better judgment. I apologize to everyone involved." But are they "truly sorry" because they did the wrong thing, or are they upset that they got caught? Let's look at two cases from the world of sports to see if we can determine the sincerity of the offending parties.

Case #1: You are relaxing in front of the television on Sunday afternoon, watching as two professional football teams compete for first place in their division. This contest aptly reflects the teams' long and sometimes bitter rivalry, which has been well-publicized by the media. Late in the hotly contested game, the camera captures one of the players deliberately kicking a downed opponent. When the offended player retaliates, a melee ensues and the referees step in to sort things out. Player A is immediately ejected from the game and shortly thereafter Player B is also sent to the showers for throwing a punch at the first player. Both athletes are really ticked off and shout a few choice expletives at the opposing team as they exit the field. Here is where our forgiveness story begins to develop.

We have the typical cast of characters in this gridiron drama—a perpetrator, a victim and a third party mediator. We expect that in a high stakes professional football game, like this one, there will always be plenty of emotion and rough play on the field, but when the final whistle blows, it's generally over. However, in this case there is some "unfinished business" between the principal actors. Still fuming at the post-game press conference, Player A alleges that Player B kicked him in the groin on the previous play and that he was only responding in kind. Videotape replays confirm his allegation and show that both players had been aggressively going at each other for most of the game. Questions begin to surface. Who is the victim? Who should apologize to whom? Did the referees handle the situation appropriately and are they now out of the picture? The bigger question to ask our readers is, "Where does forgiveness begin and end in this vignette?" Clearly, leaving the situation where it is will not yield a desirable outcome. The combatants will simply pay their fine, serve a suspension and resume their unhealthy interaction the next time they face off. Unless one of them breaks the ice and apologizes, both men (*get to*) play the role of "Victim," continuing to cast blame on someone else.[8] Isn't it true that in real life this is exactly what happens? Both sides in a dispute declare that they acted only in self-defense and doggedly maintain that they are the "good guy." Such cases never lead to reconciliation. We will return to this story later.

Case #2: We see the potential for a "convenient apology" in the case of four swimmers who represented the United States at the 2016 Olympic Games in Brazil. Ryan Lochte, a multiple gold medalist, reported that he and his teammates were returning to the Olympic Village after a party when they were pulled over and robbed at gunpoint by a group of men posing as police officers. Brazilian authorities quickly debunked the story, indicating they had surveillance video from the gas station where the alleged robbery took place that captured the athletes vandalizing a restroom. The video also showed a security guard pointing a gun at them, presumably demanding payment for damages. When another video from a popular downtown night club surfaced with footage of the Americans drinking heavily, the ruse was up on

---

[8] "Get to" is psychology speak for choosing to remain in a state of denial, a sort of mental victory over someone we are in competition with. Playing the victim provides a safety net when our ego is threatened.

Lochte's fabrications. He publicly admitted being intoxicated and "over-exaggerating" his version of events, posting this apology on his website:

> I want to apologize for my behavior last weekend—for not being more careful and candid in how I described the events of that early morning and for my role in taking focus away from the many athletes fulfilling their dreams or participating in the Olympics. I waited to share these thoughts until it was confirmed that the legal situation was addressed and it was clear that my teammates would be arriving home safely.[9]

Lochte went on to say that it was traumatic to be in a foreign country with a language barrier and then have a gun pointed at his head by an angry man demanding money. He said he accepted full responsibility for his role in the incident and claimed that he learned "some valuable lessons." The swimmer went on to thank Olympic organizers and the host country for the opportunity to compete in the Games. The immediate response from a spokesman for the Olympic Committee was one of understanding and forgiveness. Noting that Olympic athletes are under tremendous pressure, Mario Andrada excused Lochte and his teammates, saying:

> No apologies from him (Lochte) or the other athletes are needed. We need to understand that these kids were trying to have fun. Let's give these kids a break. They made a mistake. That's part of life.[10]

---

[9] Ryan Lochte, http://ryanlochte.com/#!is1/$BJSwyLJBoSH, (August 21, 2016).
[10] *Reuters*, "Rio Official: Swimmers Made a Mistake," http://www.

In an attempt to patch things up, Lochte appeared on Brazilian and American television to explain his actions in the ugly affair. Meanwhile, his corporate sponsors cancelled his lucrative endorsement contracts, reportedly amounting to more than a million dollars in annual income. As you can imagine, social media exploded with commentary, much of it in support of the apologetic Lochte and his teammates. If Ryan Lochte and the others were genuinely contrite, then forgiveness was clearly merited. However, like so many others in the same predicament, they could have been looking for "cheap grace" and a quick way out of the mess they were in. Only the swimmers know for sure.

An apology of this kind does not necessarily demand immediate forgiveness. Sometimes, a wait and see attitude is the best approach in assessing an offender's underlying convictions. In an exclusive interview on NBC, Ryan Lochte was confronted with the inconsistencies between his story and the video evidence. The emotional Lochte was unable to admit that he lied to authorities, saying that he still may have been "robbed or extorted" by the gunman. In sticking to the points of his carefully scripted press release, he was undoubtedly following the advice of his lawyers, so there may be no way of knowing how sorry Lochte is for his actions.[11]

Our society has become increasingly cynical about forced explanations for bad behavior that give the

---

nytimes.com/video/sports/olympics/100000004599474/rio-official-swimmers-made-a-mistake.html?action=click&gtype=vhs&version=vhs-heading&module=vhs&region=title-area, (August 22, 2016).

[11] On August 25, 2016, it was widely reported that Brazilian authorities had filed charges against Ryan Lochte for filing a false police report. The *New York Times* later reported that he had agreed to serve a ten-month suspension. Karen Crouse, *New York Times*, http://www.nytimes.com/2016/09/09/sports/olympics/ryan-lochte-suspended-10-months-for-rio-scandal.html?_r=0, (September 9, 2016).

appearance of inauthenticity. We note the inverse relationship between the growth of cynicism and the likelihood of forgiveness by the American public. If you doubt this, ask yourself how *you* feel when you perceive that an apology is self-serving and is being offered only because the offender was caught in the act. Because of such perceptions, Ryan Lochte will not easily be acquitted in the court of public opinion.

From our vantage point at *WisdomGuides*©, we know that thinking drives behavior, or said another way, an action is never taken without a precedent thought. If we could wave a magic wand, we would cast a "true motive" spell on the Ryan Lochte's of the world to get them to acknowledge and publicly express their real motives when they are called to account. We will offer a different version of a Lochte apology, but before we do, let's examine the "forgive and forget" attitude of the Brazilian official who dismissed the swimmers' actions by saying they were just "kids trying to have fun." His forgiving attitude could have been authentic, but it was also an astute public relations move to assure visitors that Rio de Janeiro is a safe and welcoming city. Such a gesture may have been motivated more by political expediency than by an unfeigned form of compassion. Again, we probably will never know, so let's give the official the benefit of the doubt.

The case of Ryan Lochte and his fellow swimmers dramatizes the often misunderstood nature of forgiveness and generates more questions than answers. Should Lochte be the only one to apologize? In remaining silent about their role in the alleged robbery, did Lochte's teammates also lie? Is forgiveness warranted, and if so, who should forgive the offense? Did failing to hold Lochte and the others fully accountable for their actions contribute to a better situation? The answer to this last question is, "probably not."

Now let's return to the case involving the professional football players. In a perfect world, here's what might have taken place. During an interview a few days later, Player A makes this unexpected confession: "I acted like an idiot in last Sunday's game. I let my emotions get the best of me and I was way out of line when I kicked Player B. I want to earnestly apologize to him, his teammates and the league for my inappropriate actions. I owe an apology to the fans, especially to the kids who saw what happened. I am not entirely sure what came over me, or why, but this is not the first time I have done something like this. I have taken a good, hard look in the mirror and realize that I have to stop blaming others for my problems. This morning I contacted the league office to seek professional help. I hope that everyone involved will accept my sincerest apology and count on me to be a better person moving forward."

Such an apology comes from a place of deep self-reflection and humility, and clearly Player A merits forgiveness from those he offended. He learned humility through his humiliation. Contrast his apology to the one made by Ryan Lochte. Do you think Lochte's media response and website postings reveal a man who has allowed himself to learn from his mistakes, to learn from being humiliated? Suppose he had followed Player A's lead and said, "Yes. . . yes, it's all true. We lied. We were celebrating at a night club and we drank too much. On the way back to the Olympic Village we stopped at a gas station and I vandalized the restroom. Then everything started moving really quickly. We were confused, embarrassed and afraid, so we lied about everything that happened. It was all our fault and we tried to cover it up. No excuses. I am not sure what it was inside me that prevented me from telling the truth, but it must have something to do with my life's experience and my lack of maturity. After what happened in Rio de Janeiro I realize that I have some unfinished business (pain) to deal with. Please forgive me for being such an idiot and look for a better Ryan Lochte to show up next time."

Apologies of this nature by people in the public eye are rare, but they do happen. In 2017, a heart-rending meeting took place between National Basketball Association Hall of Famers, Magic Johnson and Isiah Thomas. During their illustrious careers, the players met in two N.B.A. Finals and developed a rivalry that grew into an intense mutual hatred. It went so far that Johnson worked behind the scenes to keep Thomas off the 1992 "Dream Team" that won an Olympic Gold Medal. Thomas had previously expressed concerns that Johnson, who had been diagnosed as HIV positive, posed a danger to fellow N.B.A. players. But just before Christmas, the two men met on camera to apologize for what they had done to hurt each other. Johnson said, "You are my brother. Let me apologize if I hurt you, that we haven't been together and God is good to bring us back together." Thomas reciprocated in kind. The men tearfully hugged, expressed their love for one another and slammed the door shut on three decades of bitterness.[12]

Forgiveness is

Having tried to dispel some of the myths of what it is not, let's examine what forgiveness *is*. *Forgiveness is the art of letting go in order to find peace in your life.* Letting go is getting our pain out of the shadows and onto the table, where we can see it and name it— directly and dispassionately. Giving it a name is to tell

---

[12] Nina Mandel, *USA Today*, http://ftw.usatoday.com/2017/12/isiah-thomas-magic-johnson-emotions.View video at *Youtube.com*, https://www.bing.com/videos/search?q=magic+johnson+isiah+thomas& &view=detail&mid=6F89CF529E1A2B7D3AD96F89CF529E1A2B7D3AD9& FORM=VRDGAR, (December 20, 2017).

the truth about the hurt we feel. The people who master this art are generally among the happiest people in the world. Authentic forgiveness is a process, a series of well-defined steps toward getting right with God and with the rest of the world.

If you have visited Florence, Italy, you probably made your way to the Accademia Gallery to see the famous statue of Michelangelo's *David*. Unveiled in Florence in 1504, it is thought to be the finest extant example of High Renaissance sculpture, rising seventeen feet in height with perfect symmetry and artistic expression. Legend has it that Michelangelo, having finished sculpting his masterpiece, was surprised to find that it didn't spring to life. When asked how he was able to create such a perfect rendition of the Biblical hero, the artist explained that he saw the statue in a block of marble and simply chipped away the excess stone. That is how forgiveness works. We visualize what life would be like if we didn't have to carry around so much excess weight, and like a master craftsman, we carve away the stone that has been weighing us down.

Tom Shenk's principal occupation is in the world of corporate consulting, where he is regarded as an expert in human motivation and behavior. He has a knack for asking just the right thing at just the right moment. I have seen him pose the following disquieting question on several occasions: "What conditions have you placed on your happiness?" Invariably, what follows is an awkward silence. Tom's query is not geared to get a superficial response; on the contrary, it goes deep to the core of our emotions. Notice that Tom doesn't ask what conditions someone else has put on your happiness, he asks what conditions *you* have put on your happiness. If the responder is honest and open to self-examination, a laundry list of conditions begins to surface. Tom's is a forgiveness question and it begs personal accountability. A genuine response will come out of our past and call on those experiences that have shaped our personality and caused us to fabricate coping mechanisms to deal with our pain. Tom's question offers the gift of opportunity. The responder can elect to continue to hold onto his pain, or he can begin looking for ways to jettison some of his unwanted baggage (i.e., the conditions he places on his happiness). Not everyone is able to answer this question with candor and understanding. Some people will remain where they are for one of two reasons: either they have not learned that they are emotionally distressed because distress has become their norm; or, even when they can name their pain, they lack the tools to get out from under its weight.

We want to emphasize that we all too often put conditions on our capacity to be happy. Our goal should be to know what these conditions are and where they are coming from. Then, we can begin the process of change by forgiving ourselves for self-inflicted pain and for the pain we have inflicted on other people. There is a profound elegance to the discovery that we have hurt other people by the choices we make to remain in our personal pain.

Guidelines for forgiveness

It is said that perception defines reality, meaning what we see (or think we see) becomes our truth. English writer Douglas Adams explained this well when he observed, "Everything you see or hear or experience in any way at all is specific to you. You create a universe by perceiving it, so everything in the universe you perceive is specific to you."[13] Each of us filters life's happenings through a well-established belief system, causing us to see things from a particular vantage

---

[13] *Wikiquote*, https://en.wikiquote.org/wiki/Perception, (April 24, 2016).

point in our own private world. Because we are biased on our own behalf, our perceptions may not reflect another person's intent. It follows that we might take offense when none was intended, potentially creating a mountain out of a mole hill.

It is critical to recognize that forgiveness, while an indispensable part of the process of reconciliation, is not the same thing. *The act of forgiveness can sometimes be a one-way street, while reconciliation necessarily requires an affirmative response from the offended person(s).* This important distinction will be discussed later in the book. Meanwhile, it is essential to recognize that we can get closure even when the other person chooses not to reciprocate our overtures of forgiveness.[14]

When in doubt about forgiveness, we recommend you follow these guidelines: *a) If someone indicates that you offended them, whether you meant to or not, tell them you are sorry; b) If you (feel that you) have been offended, tell the offender in a sincere and forthright manner; c) If you think you have offended someone, but are not sure, discuss it with them as soon as possible.*

In b, above, we want the reader to understand that when you "take offense" at something another person says or does, you have *chosen* to do so. To amplify this point, when you take offense you allow the offender to gain a measure of control over your emotions.[15] More often than not, the offense comes from unfinished business in the other person, pain they have not dealt with. Why would you permit the indelicacies and poor social behavior of another person to manipulate you and "ruin your day"? In our

---

[14] Closure: the place where a person is at peace with what happened and is ready to begin living normally again.

[15] We refer here to minor offenses like unkind words or gestures that have the potential to offend. If the offense is intentional physical harm, a greater degree of recompense will be required of the offender. In this case, taking offense (feeling victimized) is clearly warranted.

professional vocabulary we refer to this as the *Why Bother Principle*, which begs the question, "Why bother to get emotionally hooked by someone else's rotten behavior?"

To live is to choose

I first came across the words "to live is to choose" in the writings of eminent Swiss physician Paul Tournier. He may not have been its originator, but Tournier's simple observation circumscribes the whole of our lives. Sometimes choosing is easy; at other times it is not. Let's see how this played out during a time when hope was all but extinguished and the capacity to choose seemed utterly incomprehensible.

Viktor Frankl was a prominent neurologist, living in Vienna during World War II. In 1942, he was identified as a Jew, captured and transported to a Nazi concentration camp. There, Frankl worked in the camp's infirmary and led efforts to establish mental health services for his fellow inmates. He managed to survive for three years in Auschwitz, Dachau and other camps before he was liberated by the Allies at the end of the war. *Man's Search for Meaning* recounts in somber detail the grim events of Frankl's life as a prisoner and outlines his principles of *Logotherapy*.[16] This was his way of coming to terms with his sufferings, while helping others to find meaning in their own ordeals. Here is what Frankl has to say about human freedom and our ability to choose:

> We who lived in concentration camps can remember the men who walked through the

---

[16] *Logotherapy* is based on Frankl's theory that man is motivated by the "will to meaning," in contrast to Freud's and Adler's materialistic theories. See: http://logotherapyinstitute.org/About_Logotherapy.html, (January 2, 2018).

huts comforting others, giving away their last piece of bread. They may have been few in number, but they offer sufficient proof that *everything can be taken from a man but one thing: the last of the human freedoms—to choose one's attitude in any given set of circumstances, to choose one's own way.*[17]

Viktor Frankl became convinced that there are choices to be made, no matter what. Every person has options, even under the most trying of circumstances. Why people choose to remain in emotional and physical distress might be a mystery to some, but not to those who have learned the art of forgiveness. Forgiveness is the most demanding—and the most liberating—action that someone can take to find happiness in their life.

We identify two categories of forgiveness, *macro* and *micro*. Opportunities for micro forgiveness arise many times during an average day, while macro forgiveness is something done on a much larger scale and by its very nature is not personal. Clearly, the Viktor Frankl story falls into the macro arena. He was imprisoned not because he was Viktor Frankl, but because he was Jewish. A micro offense, on the other hand, is distinctly personal. For example, have you ever "fought over" a parking space, or suffered a put-down at the hands of an acquaintance? Sure you have! These situations, and many others like them, represent opportunities to practice forgiveness on the micro level.

How choosing works

Tom recounts the following story, told to him many years ago by one of his business partners with the

---

[17] Viktor Frankl, *Man's Search for Meaning, An Introduction to Logotherapy* (Boston: Beacon Press: 1982), 75. Emphasis mine.

unforgettable name of Hedges Capers. On a sweltering summer afternoon, a man stopped at an ice cream parlor on his way home from work. When he got to the front of the line, the server, a young college student, held up two cones. She asked, "Chocolate or strawberry?" He answered, "Chocolate." The following verbal exchange ensued:

> *Server* asks, "Why chocolate?"
> *Man:* "Chocolate has more flavor."
>
> *Server* (holding up the cones again): "Chocolate or strawberry?"
> *Man:* "I said chocolate."
>
> *Server:* "Why?"
> *Man:* "Strawberry is too sweet!"
>
> *Server* (holding up the cones for a third time): "Chocolate or strawberry?"
> *Man* (getting a little testy): "For the last time, chocolate."
>
> *Server:* "Why?"
> *Man* (looking around for the manager): "I always order chocolate."

The server smiled and said, "Thanks for playing. Your chocolate ice cream cone is on me today." She explained that she was doing research for her Behavioral Sciences class on human patterns for making choices. She played this game with scores of customers before someone finally gave the perfect answer. Only one person in a hundred said, "Because I *choose* chocolate." Every other respondent gave an answer that had qualifiers or conditions attached to it. A few folks were irritated by the persistent questioning and one guy was mad enough to walk out empty handed. Incidentally, the college student's job was never in jeopardy. Her father owned the ice cream shop.

In the case above, the man's initial response was conditioned by the gratification he gets from eating chocolate (positive association). His next response was dictated by his dislike for strawberry ice cream (negative association). His final response came from his habit of always ordering chocolate ice cream, rather than other flavors (conditioned response). Just one customer came into the ice cream shop without conditions and simply *chose* chocolate. This is what we call being *at choice*.[18]

There is no motivation without incentive. Every human action, including destructive or negative behavior, is driven by the desire to obtain some perceived good or reward. At the point of choosing, we have a "chocolate or strawberry" decision to make. Let's say that you get into an argument with your mother and you both get angry. Later, you consider the benefits of quickly patching things up (choosing chocolate), or marinating in your misery a little longer (choosing strawberry). In choosing strawberry, you reason that winning the argument with your mother is a good thing. Winning means you won't let your mom have the satisfaction of having you make the first move toward reconciliation. At the same time, you well know that you are not always nice to your mother and you were wrong to talk to her the way you did. So, to pay for your latest indiscretion, you choose a self-inflicted punishment. You would rather eat lousy tasting strawberry ice cream than humble pie! Given the choice, you choose unhealthiness over healthiness. Why would someone do such a thing? Do you know why?

---

[18] For someone to be at choice they must be unencumbered by qualifiers and conditions, free to choose from their conscious mind (*ergo*). The conditions we place on our happiness, affecting the choices we make, come from our past experiences. To be at choice is to be fully in the present, free from the past. Being at choice, as much as is humanly possible, removes the emotions from the decision making process.

Some time ago, I received a text message from a young woman who plays for the collegiate softball team that I coach. For financial reasons, "Kelli" was still living at home with her mom and dad, while she attended school and played the game she loves. She was in a strained relationship with her parents, and if not for their financial support, Kelli would have moved out long ago. The coaching staff liked Kelli, but had been largely frustrated in their attempts to get her to leave her excess emotional baggage away from the softball diamond.

Kelli had a meltdown in a pre-season game with one of our big regional rivals. She made several errors, mostly mental ones, and our opponent jumped out to an early lead. When it became clear that Kelli's play was hurting the team's chances to stay competitive, she was pulled from the game. Earlier, she had been struck in the jaw by a hard hit ground ball, so it wasn't only her pride that was hurting. She took a seat on the bench, put an ice pack on her mouth and shut down. She was virtually inconsolable, as the game got further and further out of reach.

The following morning, I sent Kelli a text asking how she was doing. Here is what she texted back:

> I'm doing OK, Coach. Swelling went down. Still a small headache. But the amount of guilt I feel today is upsetting me. I have such a bad attitude and I know but I'm not doing anything to fix it. I'm toxic for the team like the coaches said indirectly yesterday. I want to change. But for some reason I'm letting this anger beat me.

This is a perfect example of someone who, a) consciously chooses to remain in pain, or b) is simply unable to escape from it. Her frustrations are clearly coming from her fractured relationship with her parents, who are not giving her the love and concern she yearns for.

Kelli's admission that her anger is beating her is a sure sign that she knows she's in a real battle for control of her emotions and an indication that she wishes she could make a change. She will find a cure for her anger when she begins to understand how forgiveness works. This book is being written for people just like Kelli.

During her meltdown, burdened by past failures and disappointments, Kelli was clearly not at choice. Contrast her situation with a man living in a Nazi concentration camp, a man who understood that some things were beyond his capacity to control. Viktor Frankl managed to free himself from his past and live in the here and now, where he discovered the meaning of his life in service to other human beings. *WisdomGuides*© believes that for someone to get to where Frankl and others have been, they must let go of any emotional investment in the outcome of their predicament. Sounds impossible, but it does happen, and it comes from the consciousness of a deeper reality than the one we are most familiar with. Choosing to let go is a conscious decision and is the principal reason why people are able to escape from their pain and find forgiveness in their hearts.

> *"What conditions have you placed on your happiness?"*

2

HOLE IN THE SOUL

"No problem can be solved by the same consciousness that caused it in the first place."
ALBERT EINSTEIN

Many years ago, I attended a funeral service at the First AME Church in Los Angeles, where I heard a homily by the Reverend Cecil "Chip" Murray. Pastor Murray is a riveting speaker, whose heartfelt message made a powerful impact on those in the pews that day. I can still picture him standing before the congregation and forcefully declaring, "*We are told there's a hole in the ozone, but we have holes in our souls.*" I knew the preacher was not talking about the wear and tear on my favorite loafers. No, Reverend Murray had something else in mind.

After decades of experience, we at *WisdomGuides*© have drawn certain fundamental conclusions about the nature of human beings. These conclusions lie at the heart of our mission in the world. Here is what we know. Humans are a curious amalgam of body, mind and spirit. Few people would deny the first two components. Although the third is far more elusive, we have seen too much evidence not to believe that it is real. We subscribe to the idea of the S*acred*, the spiritual dimension (Ultimate Reality) that lies beyond the material universe. What we call the "soul" is our vital, living link to the Sacred, a link that happens in intimate and mysterious ways.

We know that everyone is born with a deep longing to know the meaning of their life; to answer the question, "Why am I here?" This desire is secreted in the innermost region of our interior and to find answers takes great effort and sometimes a good deal of luck. Unfortunately, many (probably most) people fail to experience the joy of finding their highest purpose in life. *WisdomGuides©* has "*doubled down*" on our wager that a man will always find his life's meaning by serving others.

We are acutely aware that embedded in the human genome is a congenital disorder called "brokenness." Unlike illnesses of the body, brokenness is a sickness of spirit. On a daily basis, we get confirmation that most everyone carries this disease around in the form of anger, resentment, pride, jealousy and other *afflictive emotions*.[1] While the people we counsel know they have a problem, they often have no clue as to why, or what to do about it. We have also discovered that brokenness is infectious. Some folks have dealt with their issues and are in remission, but too many others are completely oblivious to what the afflictive emotions are doing to them and to those around them. Brokenness can be cured only on the highest plane of human consciousness, at the spiritual level. Spiritual brokenness was what Reverend Murray was talking about when he referred to "the hole in the soul." Unfortunately, given the choice, many people (like

---

[1] *Afflictive emotion* is a clinical term for a common human response to things that happen to us. These emotions affect our behavior and personal relationships. Afflictive emotions can be detrimental to our mental health if they are not recognized and effectively addressed.

Kelli in the previous chapter) elect not to let go of their brokenness. They continue living with a hole in their soul and don't seek the peace that one finds in *forgiven-ness*.[2]

Part and parcel of the human condition are what Cistercian monk Thomas Keating refers to as our "emotional programs for happiness."[3] Our emotional programming develops in our unconscious at an early age from our conditioning and over identification with a particular group or clan. This leads to the formation of a *false self*, or compensatory persona, which becomes representative in our dealings with the world.[4] Keating tells us that when we have an emotional investment in our instinctual needs for survival/security, affection/esteem, or power/control, events that frustrate our desires will inevitably set off one or more of the afflictive emotions. Following is a discussion of ten afflictive emotions that are endemic to the human race: anger, grief, fear, greed, envy, guilt, lust, pride, apathy and the mother of them all—shame. People in the grip of these afflictive emotions lack the capacity to forgive and get closure on the bad things that happen to them.[5]

Shame, or feeling ashamed of oneself, is the fear of disconnection and isolation. The worst thing you can

---

[2] We use the term *forgiven-ness* to describe the state of being forgiven, in contrast to *unforgiven-ness* (p. 6), the condition of one who has not sought forgiveness. Unforgiven-ness (unforgiveness) has been classified as a disease. See: Lorie Johnson, *CBN News*, "The Deadly Consequences of Unforgiveness," http://www1.cbn.com/cbnnews/healthscience/2015/June/The-Deadly-Consequences-of-Unforgiveness/, (June 22, 2015).

[3] Thomas Keating, *Invitation to Love* (New York: The Continuum Publishing Company, 1995), 20. Note: *WisdomGuides*© has been greatly influenced by Fr. Keating's keen insights into the "human condition."

[4] The *false self* is described in greater detail in the next chapter.

[5] Keating lists the afflictive emotions (numbered one to eight) among the sixteen "Levels of Consciousness" that he identifies. Number nine on his list is courage, followed by neutrality, willingness, acceptance, reason, love, joy, and peace.

tell someone, especially a child, is "Shame on you!" Translated, this message says, "You are unworthy. You're not good enough." When we feel ashamed of ourselves we lack a sense of belonging to the tribe and of being loved and cared for.

As we pointed out in the previous chapter, we put limitations on our happiness as a way of compensating for the gaps in our lives. *Anger* is a strong feeling of annoyance, frustration or hostility toward another person. Here's is an example of how anger works to throw up roadblocks on the road to happiness. I was taught to drive by my father, who was a taskmaster of the first order. He was critical of my driving, which made me hyper-sensitive about things like following too closely and failing to signal turns. To this day, I make it a point to indicate every turn and lane change I make, even when there are no other cars on the road. Dad had very little patience with mean or inconsiderate drivers, which he vociferously demonstrated to me on many occasions. Early on, I chose to adopt this aggressive reaction when encountering bad drivers. When you consider how many people tailgate and don't signal their turns, I have an almost unlimited potential to be perturbed. It's a really dumb reaction, but it has become well established in my subconscious emotional programming. Though it never ascends to the level of "road rage," my frustration with other drivers is a perfect illustration of how a person chooses to put conditions on their happiness. While on the road, I am happiest when everyone follows "Ed's Rigorous Rules of the Road."

Grief is the experience of loss; loss of a spouse, a parent, or anything we place a value on. It is the normal human reaction when someone we love dies, but it can be toxic if left unattended. How long is it appropriate (healthy) to grieve? Naturally, the loss of a material possession should not require as much grief time as the loss of a loved one. Everyone is different and each of us will have a different timeline, but here is a note of caution. One of the chief barriers to forgiving ourselves and others is unresolved grief. In times of loss, it is wise to heed the wisdom of this old saying: "One does not honor the deceased by dying with them."[6] Facing our loss with courage and resolve will always lead us to a happier place and fortify us the next time we face adversity.

Fear is triggered when our instinctual needs for survival and safety are threatened. Fear can be a healthy emotion, but it can also take over and cause us to withdraw from the flux and flow of life. When we discuss fear in the context of this book, we refer to a person's unwillingness to take the inner journey. Some of us are subconsciously fearful that we might find something out about ourselves that we don't want to know, so we choose to remain hostage to our false self.

Greed plays to our instinct for security. Greedy people never seem to have enough. Nothing will satisfy their propensity to hoard things that they may not even need. I once knew a business executive who worked his way up from nothing to become the CEO of a large company. After he made his millions, he was never satisfied with just one of something, he needed multiples of everything. If he wanted a fishing rod, he bought four. If he ran out of soap, he bought a five-year supply. Nothing fulfilled his perceived need and he never found happiness in all the stuff he stockpiled.

Envy is triggered when we compare ourselves to others. There will always be someone richer, more powerful, more successful, with a bigger house and a nicer car. After a while, comparing ourselves to others is bound to wear us out.

Guilt has many faces. Here are the three scenarios where a person should feel guilty: a) we intentionally do something wrong to harm another person; b) we

---

[6] This insightful saying comes from an unremembered source.

condone harmful acts done on our behalf by others; or, c) we fail to act when we have an opportunity to do something "good" and necessary. Interestingly, many of us feel guilty for things we could not possibly have done. For instance, feelings of empathy and compassion for the victims of racism and other forms of discrimination can become misplaced as guilt, even when we have done nothing to account for the other person's condition. Holding on to unwarranted feelings of accountability, what we call "gratuitous guilt," sustains negative perceptions we might have about ourselves. Gratuitous guilt drives us down the road to self-loathing and is certain to impede the act of self-forgiveness. Guilt in any form is a call to action; an invitation to ask for forgiveness for what we have done to feel responsible for something bad that happened.

Lust is described this way by Fr. Keating: "In the context of the frustration of the emotional programs lust refers not just to sexual misbehavior. It is the overweening desire for satisfaction, whether physical, mental, or spiritual, in order to compensate for the intolerable affronts that people have inflicted on us by not honoring our unreasonable demands."[7]

All behavior is motivated by our desire to enhance and reinforce our self-image. When we are living from the false self, *pride* strokes our ego with, "I like me just the way I am! I don't need to change a thing." When I think of how insidious pride is, I think of my friend Jackie. With a broken heart, she shared with me what happened when she visited her dying brother for the very last time. Trying to help him find a peaceful ending to his life, she pleaded with him to admit his wrongdoings and ask God for forgiveness. She explained how it had worked for her and how she found joy in her life by letting go. Jackie's brother didn't budge. His final decree to her was, "My pride won't let me." People

---

[7] Keating, *Invitation to Love*, 23.

decide to remain in *un-happiness*, even when they are at their last hour. *It takes a vision of something better for people to actually make the choice to move to a happier place in their lives.*[8]

The practical definition of "vision" is the awareness that there is something important left for us to do that will give context and meaning to our lives. Without the capacity to see down the road we will focus on trivial things and lose energy for the really important stuff, like building relationships, developing a service mentality and learning the art of forgiveness.[9]

Apathy is a terrible disease of the human spirit; it is the ultimate "cop out." People who are apathetic have thrown in the towel; they are indifferent, unconcerned and lacking in enthusiasm. Such individuals are "users," who care nothing about making the world a better place. Apathy forces them to withdraw from the rhythms of everyday life and stay (emotionally) at home to lick their wounds. A perfect example of apathy in action is found in a guy dubbed "Food Stamp Surfer Dude" on the evening news. At the time, Jason Greenslate was a twenty-something unemployed beach bum and self-styled musician from San Diego, who refused to work, relying instead on the government to take care of him. He was singled out because he used food stamps, while driving a luxury automobile. When asked by *Fox News* if he felt he was scamming the system, Surfer Dude replied, "Do I have to apologize for the way the system is set up?" He noted his contri-

---

[8] A thoroughgoing look at fear, guilt, anger, etc., as levels of human consciousness can be found in David R. Hawkins' *Power vs. Force, The Hidden Determinants of Human Behavior* (Carlsbad, CA: Hay House, 2002). Dr. Hawkins presents the case that our various states of consciousness (healthy and unhealthy) dictate our ability to discern truth from fiction.

[9] We have learned much about the power of " vision" in shaping our lives from author and lecturer Joel Barker. See: http://www.joelbarker.com/, (February 1, 2018).

bution to American society, saying, "I bring smiles to a lot of people with my music," asserting that some people were jealous because his "job is cooler than theirs." He went on to tell the interviewer that he expected to become a big rock star and earn millions of dollars. Despite his bravado, Surfer Dude is someone who has given up on himself and has propped up a pleasing caricature in his place. People like Greenslate are not who they say they are. They purport to love themselves, but it is the image of someone else they are in love with. Apathetic people despise who they really are.[10]

Not listed among the afflictive emotions are two other factors that have a bearing on our emotional programs for happiness—*ignorance* and *self-deception*. Ignorance allows us to swim blissfully along like a frog in the warm water of the stove pot, never conscious that it is being boiled.[11] Tom once attended a four-day workshop where pioneering management and total quality expert W. Edwards Deming was the leader. On the first day of the workshop, the facilitator introduced Dr. Deming and encouraged anyone with a question to use one of several microphones set up around the meeting room. After about an hour, a member of the audience approached a microphone and was recognized. When he spoke, Deming effectively ignored him, which made the man feel like "a fool." Unsure of what to make of it, he silently wandered back to his seat. A little later, as Deming shifted to a different topic, a young woman strode confidently to the microphone and was called on. Her question met with the very same disinterested response, which made her

---

[10] *Fox News*, "Jesse Watters Meets the Food Stamp Surfer Dude," http://nation.foxnews.com/2014/02/25/jesse-watters-meets-food-stamp-surfer-dude, (February 24, 2014).
[11] This is the popular "boiling frog" metaphor, used to illustrate how undetected incremental changes in our environment may lead to dramatic results.

feel foolish as well. The woman pushed back, saying "Dr. Deming, you don't have to be so rude. I was simply asking for clarification." Deming persisted in evading her question. When a third person tried his luck, he also received the same treatment. Tom sensed he was in for a true learning moment and was anxious to see what Deming's next move would be. He had to wait until the following afternoon when an intrepid soul approached the microphone and began his inquiry with, "Dr. Deming I would appreciate an answer to my question without an inappropriate and rude attack." Deming loudly interrupted and with great energy in his voice he asked the young man, "How can you know?" Despite the efforts of several subsequent questioners, this became the standard response for the rest of the afternoon. On the following day, Dr. Deming changed his tone and his answer became, "Now that you know. . ." Deming closed the workshop with these words: "Now that you know, don't be a fool." It was then that Tom clearly understood what Deming was teaching them through his measured responses. He was boiling frogs.

This story fits intriguingly into our forgiveness paradigm. In marking his questioners as fools, Deming did not intend personal attacks, but was giving his audience a dose of honesty about their personal shortcomings. The "How can you know?" response was Deming's call to humility. It's OK to not know. So forgive yourself and heed Deming's final admonition: "Now that you know, don't be a fool." If you're reading this book, don't be foolish. Learn as much as you can about yourself and about how you fit into the world around you. Then put that knowledge to good use. . . or you really are a fool.

Self-deception is the step-child of ignorance. Not having learned any other escape from our problems, we deceive ourselves into believing that everything is just fine and that our biggest problems will work themselves out. Thus, we never see ourselves as complicit in what's gone wrong with our lives. Cistercian monk Thomas Merton was surely talking about such deception when he observed: "We are not very good at recognizing illusions, least of all the ones we cherish about ourselves."[12] It is a vicious circle, wherein ignorance breeds self-deception, which nourishes pridefulness, which in turn compounds ignorance.

Among Tom's provocative observations, is this: *"A man cannot get enough of what he does not want."* What does this mean and why is it so important for us to recognize that, among other things, no amount of alcohol or drugs or working overtime at the office will ever satisfy our deepest longings for love, attention and connectedness? These things only serve to feed our afflictive emotions and deepen our spiritual emptiness. Consider the person who has never felt the love of a parent (this is the big one!). Although she wishes the hurt and the guilt would go away, the victim simply cannot find enough strength to deal with her problem. She finds a "remedy" in drugs and alcohol, an outward manifestation of the need to relieve her inward pain. Before long she is in the clutches of something that is guaranteed not to help, and sadly she knows it. She becomes addicted to the "fix," which masks her deeper longing to receive love and affection from her mother and father. She cannot get enough of what she does not really want, or need.

As human beings, we desire happiness and yearn to know why we are here. Permit us to draw once more on the wit and wisdom of Mark Twain. He says, "The two most important days in your life are the day you are born, and the day you find out why."[13] Twain cleverly

---

[12] Thomas Merton, *Seeds of Contemplation* (Norfolk, CT: New Directions Books, 1949), 28.

[13] This quote is generally attributed to Twain. See: *Wikiquote,* https://en.wikiquote.org/wiki/Mark_Twain, (January 22, 2016).

posits that every life comes with a purpose, to which we are sure, Viktor Frankl would heartily agree. No one finds the purpose for his life in a brothel or at the bottom of a whiskey bottle. No one cures his brokenness by lighting up another joint or by wagering his paycheck in a Las Vegas casino. Only God can fill the hole in our soul; only God can make us whole.

Filling the hole

So, what does it look like when God fills our soul's hole? Here is a dynamic example that comes from a model for sober living developed in the early 1930's by way of the friendship of two hopeless drunks from Vermont. The story winds its way through a series of fortuitous meetings between desperate men and those who would eventually lead them to freedom. Let's begin with a man named Rowland H.

Rowland was a well-heeled member of a prominent Rhode Island family, who was near the breaking point. He had tried everything to try to stop drinking, but nothing worked. As a last resort, he traveled to Switzerland to consult Dr. Carl Jung, regarded as the father of modern analytical psychology. After meeting with him, Jung concluded that Rowland's condition was irreversible. Believing that the spiritual life is important to man's well-being, he directed Rowland to a religious outreach he knew of, called the Oxford Group. Before departing, Jung told him that only a "vital spiritual experience" could create the conditions for his cure.[14]

The Oxford Group had been founded in 1928 by Frank Buchman and others. Buchman was a Pennsylvania born Lutheran minister, who was something of a religious zealot. He traveled extensively, pursuing

---

[14] See Alcoholics Anonymous for valuable information on its history. http://www.aa.org/pages/en_US/aa-timeline, (January 21, 2016).

his ambition to rescue as many souls as he could from the trash heap of life and lead them to eternal salvation. After his ordination in 1902, Buchman worked as director of the Y.M.C.A. at Penn State College, and then as a missionary to China. He subsequently took a post at Hartford Theological Seminary, where he was active in forming Christian student groups at Yale and Princeton Universities. Driven by wanderlust, he left Hartford and took up the life of an itinerant evangelist, holding "house parties" wherever he went. The name "Oxford Group" was derived from the meetings that Buchman regularly held in the Oxford University Chapel in the late 1920's.

Acting on Dr. Jung's advice, Rowland began attending Oxford Group meetings and before long he enthusiastically adopted their spiritual methods of recovery. This time his efforts paid off and he was able to permanently quit drinking. Rowland's remarkable turnaround inspired another Oxford Group member named Ebby. Carrying the good news of Rowland's triumph, Ebby traveled to New York and sought out his old friend Bill W., an alcoholic with a long history of failed attempts at sobriety. Ebby tried to persuade him to join the Oxford Group, but Bill remained a skeptic and a drunk. Then in December 1934, while in the hospital for treatment, he had an epiphany—a spiritual encounter with his brokenness that was unlike anything he had ever experienced before. Suddenly, the dark cloud that shrouded his life lifted and Bill never touched another drink.

Through the Oxford Group, Bill was introduced to Dr. Bob S., an Akron surgeon with a heart for service. The two men hit it off and began working with alcoholics at the local hospital. Meanwhile, they launched other support groups in Cleveland and New York. By the time the name "Alcoholics Anonymous" came to be associated with the movement, more than a hundred souls had been cured of their addiction to alcohol. Using its group therapy approach, A.A. became the first organization to effectively deal with alcoholism on such a large scale. Untold millions of people have led happy and fulfilling lives, owing to the remarkable commitment of these two dedicated men and others who followed in their footsteps. Here is the twelve-step program of A.A.:[15]

1. We admitted we were powerless over alcohol—that our lives had become unmanageable.

2. Came to believe that a Power greater than ourselves could restore us to sanity.

3. Made a decision to turn our will and our lives over to the care of God *as we understood Him*.

4. Made a searching and fearless moral inventory of ourselves.

5. Admitted to God, to ourselves, and to another human being the exact nature of our wrongs.

6. Were entirely ready to have God remove all these defects of character.

7. Humbly asked Him to remove our shortcomings.

8. Made a list of all persons we had harmed, and became willing to make amends to them all.

9. Made direct amends to such people wherever possible, except when to do so would injure them or others.

10. Continued to take personal inventory and when we were wrong promptly admitted it.

---

[15] The name "Oxford Group" was changed to "Moral Re-Armament" (M.R.E.) in 1938. With the war in Europe, Buchman sought a global moral recovery and wanted the name of the organization to reflect its aims.

11. Sought through prayer and meditation to improve our conscious contact with God, *as we understood Him*, praying only for knowledge of His will for us and the power to carry that out.

12. Having had a spiritual awakening as the result of these Steps, we tried to carry this message to alcoholics, and to practice these principles in all our affairs.[16]

The twelve-step model is based largely on the precepts of the Oxford Group. It relies heavily on forgiveness—God's forgiveness, self-forgiveness and the forgiveness of others. As you will discover, this directly correlates with the formula for a happy life we prescribe here in this book.

Courage to forgive

There is more to tell about Frank Buchman and the courage it takes to confront our mistakes and begin the process of reconciliation. Buchman was again working for the Young Men's Christian Association when he accepted a call to ministry in Overbrook, a small suburb of Philadelphia. Overbrook had no church building, so he rented an old downtown store front to provide worship space and give him a place to live. While traveling abroad, Buchman hit on the idea of establishing a hostel for the mentally ill when he got back to Philadelphia. Upon his return home, however, he was deeply disappointed to find that the board of directors was unwilling to fund his project. A contentious dispute ensued and he quit his post. Bitter over his resignation, he was advised by his doctor to take a vacation. While traveling in England, he was

---

[16] Copyright © 1952, 1953, 1981 by Alcoholics Anonymous Publishing, now known as Alcoholics Anonymous World Services, Inc.

struck by a great spiritual upheaval. This is how he described what happened:

> I thought of those six men back in Philadelphia who I felt had wronged me. They probably had, but I'd got so mixed up in the wrong that I was the seventh wrong man. I began to see myself as God saw me, which was a very different picture than the one I had of myself. I don't know how you explain it, I can only tell you I sat there and realized how my sin, my pride, my selfishness and my ill-will, had eclipsed me from God. . . I was the center of my own life. That big "I" had to be crossed out. I saw my resentments against those men standing out like tombstones in my heart. I asked God to change me and He told me to put things right with them. It produced in me a vibrant feeling, as though a strong current of life had suddenly been poured into me and afterwards a dazed sense of a great spiritual shaking-up.[17]

Buchman buried the "tombstones in his heart" and immediately wrote warm letters of apology to each of the estranged board members. The "seventh wrong man" got back in God's good graces and back into right relationship with other men. It took courage, but he confronted his demons (his afflictive emotions) and did the right thing. Here is what one of his letters read:

> Am writing, to tell you that I have harbored an unkind feeling toward you—at times I conquered it but it always came back. Our views may differ but as brothers we must love. I write to ask your forgiveness and to assure that I love you and trust by God's grace I shall

---

[17] Garth Lean, *Frank Buchman, A Life* (London: Constable & Robinson, Ltd., 1985), 30.

never more speak unkindly or disparagingly of you.[18]

Frank Buchman became an activist for global peace, preaching a message of love and compassion around the world. Along the way he made many friends, including the likes of Mahatma Gandhi and other national leaders. During World War II, he worked tirelessly to convert Nazis to Christianity, admonishing them to seek the Almighty's forgiveness for their sins. His efforts did not go unnoticed, and when the war ended he was decorated with the French *Légion d'honneur* and the *Order of Merit of the Federal Republic of Germany*. Not surprisingly, Frank Buchman recognized his dramatic moment of forgiveness and reconciliation as the turning point of his life.

Steps to forgiven-ness

As was outlined earlier, the term forgiven-ness is used to describe a state of being wherein we find peace in knowing that we stand in right relationship with God and with our fellow human beings. We propose that we get to forgiven-ness through four stages:

1. *Spiritual level:* Ask God for forgiveness for what we have done to hurt him and others; and forgiveness for things we should have done, but did not.

2. *Personal level:* Forgive ourselves for being so utterly human.

3. *Relationship level:* Forgive those who have hurt us. This may mean, forgive those whom *we allow* to hurt us.

---

[18] Ibid., 31.

4. *Level of Reconciliation:* Ask forgiveness from those whom we have hurt.

Real forgiveness happens at the deepest level of consciousness, in *Godspace*. Remember, this book makes no attempt to tell you who God is; you make that determination for yourself, based on your individual experience. If you are more comfortable with the idea of a "Higher Power," that's perfectly fine. Irrespective of the way you come to know your Higher Power, the important thing is that you recognize how helpless you are without his help.

We are convinced that forgiveness works best when the four stages are done in sequence. We don't think that you can arrive at the place of self-forgiveness, unless you have first asked for mercy from the Creator. You surely can't unconditionally forgive another person, without having seen in them the reflection of your own brokenness. And, you will not genuinely ask another person for forgiveness until you have been humbled by the insights you gained in self-examination.

Your relationships can be represented by a simple triangle, where God, your fellow humans and you are positioned at the three points. Interaction and communication occur bilaterally in the tension between these points. We interface with other inhabitants of planet Earth on a measurable two-dimensional plane of time and space, but what about our connection to God? Such a relationship must happen at a deeper (celestial, spiritual) level, and is difficult—some say impossible—to quantify.

On the following page are two figures which represent our triangular connections. The solid lines in Figure 1a indicate healthy relationships between you, God and other persons. The arrows show that there is mutual communication happening through these connections.

Relationship Triangle©
(Healthy)

```
         God
          ▲
         ╱ ╲
        ╱   ╲
    Celestial
      (spirit)
- - - - - - - - - - - - -
    (space / time)
    Terrestrial
   ╱           ╲
 You ◄────────► Others
```

Figure 1a

Figure 1b illustrates what happens when you deliberately do something to harm another person.

Relationship Triangle©
(Unhealthy)

```
         God
          ▲
   💥  Celestial
         (spirit)
- - - - - - - - - - - - -
      (space / time)
       Terrestrial
            💥
 You ◄────────► Others
```

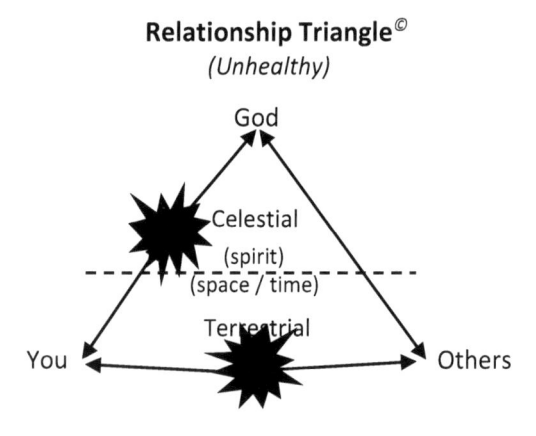

Figure 1b

Actions that fracture the human to human connection also create a rift with God. This is the part of the story that your therapist probably can't (or won't) tell you. Accountability for ill actions, what we know as "sin," goes above and beyond the earthly requirement to make amends, and in these cases the perpetrator must appeal to a higher authority to make restitution and achieve a full reconciliation. This understanding of forgiveness is where the secular psychologist parts company with the believer in a Higher Power.

The first step

Take a moment to think about the Einstein quote at the top of this chapter: "No problem can be solved by the same consciousness that caused it in the first place." Richard Rohr tells us, "In the first half of life, the negative, the mysterious, the scary, and the problematic are always exported elsewhere." This gives us a "quick and firm ego structure," says Rohr, but it "is not an objective statement of truth." We must rise to a new level of understanding (insight) to see how we have overcompensated by hiding things that happened in our past. Unless we consciously integrate all the scary stuff into our personal narrative, we are doomed to live a divided life, alienated from the truth of who we really are. Rohr calls this integration of hidden truth, "the forgiveness of everything."[19]

True and lasting forgiveness of any kind can be achieved only after we surrender to a Power greater than us. The best place to petition God for mercy is in solitude and in silence. Begin by finding a quiet space and simply listening for the "still, small voice" that abides within each one of us. If you cannot hear the gentle pulse of your soul, focus on a sacred word like "peace" or "Mother" or "Father." Silently repeat the word over and over until it starts to block out all the

---

[19] Franciscan friar Richard Rohr is the founder of the Center for Action and Contemplation in Albuquerque, New Mexico. He writes poignantly on how Einstein's statement applies, not just to scientific research, but also to human behavior. See: Richard Rohr, *Falling Upward, A Spirituality of the Two Halves of Life* (San Francisco: Jossey-Bass, 2011), 10–13, 148.

other messages triggered in your head. Continue to make a habit of quiet time dedicated to prayer and contemplation. If you are struggling in this effort. . . wait. You might be surprised by what shows up when you are receptive to a "*new see*" in your life. If we are going to turn up the scary stuff buried in our past, it's going to require some serious excavation. Following are some proven methods for digging in just the right places.

Journaling is the practice of recording your thoughts and feelings in a notebook or sheet of paper. We encourage people to use the old fashioned method of hand writing their journal, rather than using a keyboard. There seems to be something particularly revealing when you see your hand crafting words on a page. However, the computer will probably always remain the preferred method for many of us. The idea is to keep writing, even if it seems frivolous and unproductive at times. One day, journaling will be a "data dump" of all the mental and emotional flotsam in your mind; the next day it becomes a record of your most intimate thoughts and feelings. Journaling creates synergy between your heart and your head, revealing things about you that may not have drifted into your consciousness before. This practice has proven to be good therapy for many people we know. Some of them go back to their journals, perhaps years later, and remember what they were once thinking and feeling. Mystics refer to this place of self-revelation as *liminal space*, or the place where we are most vulnerable to learning about our deeper selves.

Reflective reading is an effective technique that *WisdomGuides*© uses to open folks up to the voice of the Spirit. Here is how it works. Select an appropriate "wisdom reading" and carefully read a chosen passage, making notes on those things that register with you as interesting and insightful. Then, re-read the same section. You may even want to read it a third time, or a fourth. When you have finished, ask yourself the following questions: "What struck me most about the reading?"; "Where do I see myself in the reading?"; "What did I learn about myself?" Then make notes, pausing and waiting for the still, small voice to enter the conversation.[20]

Forgiveness manifesto

Almost anyone you meet in the western world has read at least some of the Holy Bible. For some, the Bible is nothing more than a fictional account of a bunch of religious fanatics and their followers who wandered around the Sinai desert a few thousand years ago. This outlook, however, does not do justice to the remarkable stories of love and honor and courage and faith that one finds in the pages of this ancient text. You do not have to be an expert to gain insight from the accounts of the men and women in the Biblical narrative. Scripture gives us a whole panorama of forgiveness. Indeed, it is the truest manifesto of forgiveness that we know of.

The principal figure in the New Testament is, of course, Jesus Christ. Whatever you think about Jesus, the words of wisdom attributed to him are, to say the least, uncommon. He says things like, "Love your enemies."[21] "Unless you change and become like a little child, you won't get to heaven."[22] and "If you have a high opinion of yourself, you're going down. Lowly people will be the winners."[23] C'mon, who says things like that? Whether you regard him as a prophet, the

---

[20] A list of wisdom literature can be found on page 192.
[21] Matt., 5:44.
[22] Ibid., 18:3. This quote and the one immediately following are our interpretations.
[23] Ibid., 23:12.

son of God, or someone else, Jesus can really get under your skin.

Perhaps the most troubling Biblical account of forgiveness occurs with Jesus dying on a wooden cross. Picture this: Jesus said, "Father, forgive them, for they do not know what they are doing."[24] So, Jesus did what he exhorted everyone else to do. He loved his enemies and implored God to forgive them, even after they tortured him, pounded a crown of thorns into his skull and nailed him to a tree to die in agony. The story gets even better. There were two criminals hanging next to him on their own trees. One of them cynically said to Jesus, "You're a fraud! You can't even save yourself from dying." In contrast to his impenitent friend, however, the second bad guy was filled with remorse for all the evil things he had done. In a movie version, his conversation with Jesus would probably go something like this, "Jesus, I believe you are who they say you are. I now realize how much pain and suffering I have caused in my life. Will you forgive me for my sins?" Jesus' response is recorded. He said, "Truly, I tell you, today you will be with me in Paradise."[25] More than a few Biblical scholars have anguished over the significance of this passage.

This whole scene is rife with symbolism. Here is this paragon of mercy, whose last act before dying is to forgive everyone who collaborated in his demise. Then we have the archetypical scenario of two men who are faced with a difficult decision—to die in forgiven-ness, or to remain in the darkness. To live is to choose. Only one of the men chooses life. It is an easy call as to which of these bad guys died in peace.

Perhaps the choice given these men is the same one we have to make. We can choose to continue to be governed by our afflictive emotions, or we can come out

---

[24] Luke, 23:34.
[25] Ibid., 23:43.

into the light and ask God (our Higher Power) for forgive-ness. This is the first step toward living in the place of peace, in the land of the forgiven.

> *What would it take for you to ask God for forgiveness?*

3

THE ENEMY IS US

"One learns humility only through humiliation."
WISDOMGUIDES©

Renowned cultural anthropologist Ernest Becker writes, "Man is the only animal who laughs or cries, because he is the only animal who knows the difference between the way things are and the way things ought to be."[1] Being human is both a blessing and a curse. Man's glory is his unique ability to see himself in the context of creation, in the vast landscape of history, but he is vexed by the knowledge that he lives in an imperfect world. Humans are fated to live in tension between their hopes and dreams at one end and the sobering realities of Earthly life on the other.

What then does it mean to be truly human? Because life is not fair, we are guaranteed to experience pain and suffering along the way. We can suffer in a thousand ways—physically, mentally, emotionally and

---

[1] Ernest Becker, *The Denial of Death* (New York: The Free Press, 1973), from the summary on the inside flap. Becker pioneered multi-disciplinary research linking science, the humanities, social action and religion.

spiritually. Suffering often involves (results from interaction with) other people, but don't we bring much of it upon ourselves?

We all have an *ego*, which is our first line of defense against our trials and tribulations. In its simplest terms, the ego is our sense of self (self-importance) in relation to the world outside. If fed the wrong diet, the ego can grow to monstrous proportions, giving us a distorted self-image. This is our *false*, or *ego-self*, and if left unchecked this imposter takes on a life of its own, effectively obscuring our view of who we really are. This obfuscation can become the biggest hurdle we must leap over on the way to a happy life. The false self deceives us into believing that we are better than we really are; that there is nothing wrong and that we don't need to play the forgiveness game. The territory of the false self is fertile soil for pridefulness, envy and greed.

The *True Self*, on the other hand, is the locus of authenticity and integrity. When we go deeper and get in touch with our True Self, we position ourselves for positive life changes—changes that happen only in humbleness. Being human is to live with two competing and contradictory selves.[2]

Suffering in humility

Webster's dictionary says that humiliation is experienced when someone is "made to feel very ashamed, or foolish."[3] Unfortunately, the only proven way to get to forgiven-ness is to be knocked down, dragged through the mud and have the hell beat out of you. I'm

---

[2] Esoteric Science gives a useful synopsis of the *true-self*, the *false self* and the *ego* at its website, http://www.esotericscience.org/articlea.htm, (February 2, 2016).

[3] *Merriam-Webster* is the principal online source for word definitions used in this book.

referring not to physical assault, but to the beating our ego takes when we realize that we aren't as good as we thought we were. The best person to make us feel ashamed of ourselves is. . . us. If you want to be humble, you're going to have to suffer through humiliation.

The people we work with at *WisdomGuides*© have learned that, no matter how much we try to avoid it, humiliation happens. It might be in the form of something stupid we say to a neighbor, or when we look at the time and realize that we missed an appointment with our best client. Humiliation results when we forget to pay the credit card bill on time, or when our wife asks, "Honey, do you remember what day it is?" You get the idea. Humiliation is pretty much a daily occurrence for most of us.

There is a *WisdomGuides*© prayer that goes like this, "Lord, please let today's humiliations come early, so that I can learn from them today and not take them to bed with me tonight, where they will cause me to lose sleep. Amen." A petition like this can originate only from someone who has a healthy awareness of self.

Forgiving yourself is probably the hardest thing you will ever attempt. The incapacity to forgive one's self is the main reason why people can't forgive others. This is why people like David in Chapter One are stuck in the mud, unable to dig themselves out from under their burdensome egos. This is why people take drugs, drink too much, even take their own lives. Self-forgiveness has a favorable flip side, though. Because it is so difficult, it renders an almost euphoric feeling of joy when it is finally accomplished. No pain, no gain! No big pain, no big gain!

Forgiveness in the wild

As we noted in the preceding chapter, the best starting

point to begin the process of forgiveness is alone in pure silence. If you want to experience the healing forces of nature in your soul, try venturing into the profound silence of the wilderness. Wisdom abounds in her quiet contemplative space, where a man is gently guided toward a place where he can see the truth about himself; where he learns humility. The following is my account of how I came face-to-face with my demons and got the hell beat out of me.

I had been happily employed with the Procter & Gamble Company for nearly twenty-four years. I was in my middle forties, with a wife, two children and a heap of financial obligations. On a fateful October morning in 1996, I was given notice that my job was being eliminated, and for the first time in my life I felt unwanted and unloved. Numbed with fear, I took the downward trail into darkness.

After the initial shock and a period of denial and disbelief, I entered the abyss of anger and resentment. A man can lose his way in such cold and forbidding places. I was on a lonely journey, but through counseling and the encouragement of family and friends, I slowly began to claw my way back to emotional well-being. Though I had scarcely picked up a book since my college days, I began reading voraciously. In the year following my job loss, I read more than a hundred books, cover to cover—philosophy, science, nature, history, theology—anything dealing with truth and significance. I began spending an increasing amount of time in contemplation, searching for the meaning of my life.

As I had so often done in my youth, I sought the solitude of the mountains. I sometimes went flyfishing for the day to the upper reaches of the Kern River, which is just a three-hour drive from the Los Angeles area. I have fished some of the finest rivers and streams in North America, but the Kern tops my list. For miles on end the cold crystal clear water pours over stones of endless shapes and colors—shimmering shades of red and yellow and green. The flatter sections of the river are made up of broad emerald pools, some as much as eighty feet across. But in the narrows of the canyons, the current rips across polished granite with incredible ferocity, belying the sense of calm that one gets from the shoreline. In springtime the Kern can be treacherous, but by mid-summer she is transformed into a dry-fly fisherman's paradise. The Kern is a dangerous place, but it is also where a man can recover his soul.

It was early June and I left home before dawn to drive to Kernville, the small town stepping off point for rafters, hikers and fishermen. After a hot breakfast in the local coffee shop, I traveled the remaining twenty miles along the river until I reached the parking lot at the Johnsondale Bridge. It was mid-week and there were only a couple of cars in the lot, meaning I wouldn't have much company along the river. Perfect!

After hiking along the river trail for an hour or so, I assembled my rod, tied on my favorite fly pattern and waded out into the current. As it usually does, it took me a few minutes to get my casting rhythm going, but before long I was right in sync. Then, suddenly and without warning, I was overcome with emotion. I found myself tearfully murmuring these three words: "You're still here! You're still here!" I had been slowly, unknowingly absorbed into the beauty around me. Everything seemed to downshift into low gear. I was in ultra-slow motion. It was as if a peace was flowing into me and I was becoming part of the river itself. Though I was present in time and space, I had somehow transcended it. I do not know how else to describe what happened, except to say that I have never experienced anything in my life that was so deeply moving.

On the trip home, I had plenty of time to reflect on the events of the day. Though I couldn't pinpoint exactly what it was, something felt different. After that, there was a big shift in my outlook on life. It was not long before I found my dream job and enjoyed a wonderful career, immersed in service to other people. I was a happy person again and as a result my relationships improved noticeably. I became more active in community and church affairs, where I started giving back, instead of being so focused on myself. The stars were back in alignment and everything was right with the world once more.[4]

It is hard for me to believe that more than two decades have passed since that unforgettable experience. In preparing to write this book, I finally got around to unpacking the significance of what happened that day on the Kern River. Many times, from the depths of my depression, I cried out God to forgive me for the many mistakes I had made in my life. Then, he answered me in the stillness of the canyon and in a single precious moment all the garbage that I had been dragging around for such a long time was swept away by the river of life.

My walk into the light of forgiven-ness might never have happened had I not ventured into the world of nature. Nature reboots our systems and gets us functioning again in the way God intended. She has a way of drawing us in with her beauty, then seducing us back into the mainstream. One fine day long ago, she helped me to rediscover my path to happiness. Nature opened up my heart and I forgave myself for everything.

Humility versus hubris

To say it one more time, the single biggest factor in coming to forgiveness is humility. Here is what the

---

[4] Edwin L. Andersen, *Lessons of the Wild, Learning from the Wisdom of Nature* (Eugene, OR: Wipf & Stock, 2009), 56–8.

inimitable C. S. Lewis has to say about it: "True humility is not thinking less of yourself, it's thinking of yourself less." Anyone who would say that he is a "humble person" is kidding himself. Humility is one of those things that, just when you think you've got it, you have less of it than you had before.

The converse of humility is hubris, or pridefulness. Pride is produced by our egos, i.e. the opinion we have of ourselves in relation to the world outside. The more self-important we become, the more likely we are to be prideful. Naturally, you should be proud of your daughter for getting accepted into a top university, but beware of taking credit for her achievement. It is appropriate to be grateful when you get a promotion at the office, but don't start giving yourself pats on the back, or you will let pride sneak in through the back door.

Recently, I had a "come to Jesus" meeting with a young man from one of the small groups that Tom and I facilitate. By every worldly measure of success, "Scott" gets high marks. He's intelligent and good-looking, has a beautiful wife and two sons, lives in a nice home and does very well financially. Despite outward appearances, we suspected that Scott was hiding something. It was not until we got to know him better that we realized his problems were bigger than we first imagined. We learned that Scott was an alcoholic and that his marriage was careening down a dead end road. He was trying to keep himself from spinning out of control by denying what was happening and continuing full speed ahead. To protect his ego, he characterized himself as the "Incredible Hulk," a blow-up man capable of withstanding anything people could hit him with. In his personal life, the Hulk became Scott's go-to guy, his first and last line of defense. The Hulk was larger than life and he had developed a gigantic ego.

In one of our face-to-face sessions, I asked the Hulk—I mean Scott—to rate the other men in his peer group, based on how humble he thought they were. Using a ten point scale, where zero is complete absence of ego (humility) and ten is ego saturation (pridefulness), Scott rated his colleagues. I did the same. We compared notes and briefly discussed how we arrived at our scores, which ranged from three to eight. I then asked him to rate himself using the same rubric. There was no reason for me to be surprised when Scott declared himself to be "about a four," but I was. I guessed that he would give himself a six, or higher, especially given the circumstances.

When I told him, "Scott, I rate you a ten on the pride-o-meter," the look on his face was worth a million words. I sensitively told Scott what I saw in him to persuade me that he had a self-image problem. It was a pretty hard blow for the Hulk to absorb, but I gambled that he would respond in a positive way. At the next group meeting, he confessed, "I am starting to see that I have a lot of pride. I am working on it." Awareness is the first step to overcoming a problem. Scott knows he has a ton of work to do, but he is willing to try to make things better for himself and his family.

The exalted shall be humbled

Authentic forgiveness at any level requires that we leave pride at the door. During the 2016 presidential primaries, *Fox News* aired a spirited exchange between then candidate Donald Trump and talk show host Bill O'Reilly. Both men are eminently successful in their chosen professions, but neither is known for his great humility. Admittedly, it takes a well-developed ego to survive in the arenas where they make their living, but both men would undoubtedly give the pride-o-meter a pretty good jolt.

Mr. Trump had unexpectedly announced that he would not participate in the final Republican debate, hosted by *Fox News*. He implied that the reason for his withdrawal was that he was "not treated well by *Fox*" in a prior debate. In the interview, O'Reilly pointed out, "In your Christian faith, there is a very significant tenet, and that's the tenet of forgiveness. I think you should forgive, not only journalists who come at you in ways you don't like, but I think you should be the bigger man. . . don't you think that's the right thing to do?" Trump glibly responded, "It probably is, but it's called an eye for an eye . . ."[5]

Initially, Bill O'Reilly's plea to Donald Trump seemed fairly reasonable. But, let's dig a little deeper. When O'Reilly bought up the fact that they had known each other for thirty-five years, Trump nodded in agreement. O'Reilly knew that Trump was not about to apologize, and if he did, it would probably be for reasons other than pure contrition. You can also be sure that O'Reilly was keenly aware that his employer's television ratings would be much lower if Trump was not on the stage for the debate. The talk show host even went so far as to try to embarrass Trump, by saying, "You went to church last Sunday. You don't usually go." At best, O'Reilly was being disingenuous in trying to goad Trump into changing his mind.[6]

---

[5] Bill O'Reilly, http://www.billoreilly.com/show?action=latestTVShow#1, (January 26, 2016).

[6] Subsequent to this writing, Mr. O'Reilly was dismissed from *Fox News*, amid claims of sexual harassment by several female coworkers. It was reported that a total of $13MM had been paid out to prevent lawsuits against O'Reilly and the network. Liam Mathews, *TV Guide*, "Bill O'Reilly Fired From Fox News," http://www.tvguide.com/news/bill-oreilly-fired-fox-news/, (April 19, 2017).

Here is the question that *Fox News'* Megyn Kelly asked Trump at the prior debate, which led to his withdrawal:

> Mr. Trump, one of the things people love about you is you speak your mind and you don't use a politician's filter. However, that is not without its downsides, in particular, when it comes to women. You've called women you don't like 'fat pigs,' 'dogs,' 'slobs,' and 'disgusting animals.'[7]

While not denying the accusations, Trump responded that he didn't remember calling women such things. Apparently, this was not the first time that he and Kelly had clashed. Since he did not receive the apology he felt was due, Trump might seem justified in holding his ground. He openly admitted that he pulled out of the debate to get back at the network.

Pridefulness is in full bloom in this war of words. Everyone made a choice to keep at least one foot in the mire of their afflictive emotions. We had a business mogul with a full ego, who chose to take the bait (pride is hurt) when a female journalist he dislikes tried to offend him. When confronted, the journalist elected not to soften her stance (must win) and the news network backed her all the way (choosing not to be pushed around). Big ego surrogate Bill O'Reilly entered the conversation and presumed to mediate the dispute by playing the "shame game." He resoundingly failed. When you add up all the hubris on display in this public relations nightmare there were no winners. Nothing appeared to be authentic about the personal

---

[7] Aaron Blake, *The Washington Post*, "Here are the Megyn Kelly Questions that Donald Trump is Still Sore About," https://www.washingtonpost.com/news/the-fix/wp/2016/01/26/here-are-the-megyn-kelly-questions-that-donald-trump-is-still-sore-about/, (January 28, 2016).

interactions; the players were combative, defensive and self-oriented. Personal accountability went out the window and everyone lost. Once again, prominent public figures succeeded in moving us away from an attitude of civility and cooperation, exacerbating the political and social polarization of our times.

Who needs it?

One of the maxims we live by in our professional endeavors is this: "*More harm is caused by those who take offense, than by those who give offense.*" What does it mean to "take offense" at something done to us or said about us? And, why do some people choose to be offended, while others do not? Recognizing that all behavior is designed to enhance or reinforce our self-image, it is easy to see why people do and say hurtful things. By their words and actions they (consciously, or not) try to manipulate others in order to get what they want and feel better about themselves. In choosing to be offended, people who are targets of these manipulations advertise to the world that they have unfinished business, unresolved personal conflicts that make them vulnerable. On the other hand, persons who have a healthy self-image are better equipped to see an undeserved verbal attack as nothing more than a veiled attempt at manipulation and *self-projection*.[8] Such persons choose not to fall victim to the attacker; they know the attack is not about them, so they choose not to be offended. Rather than internalizing it, they look for alternative solutions to repair and rebuild the relationship.

---

[8] *Self-projection* is an unconscious defense mechanism, used to project our unwanted feelings toward another person. In this way, a person denies their negative sub-conscious impulses and qualities by foisting them onto others.

We sometimes hear people say, "I lead a good life. I'm on good terms with everyone. I don't need to forgive anyone. I have already done that." As they look at the home page of their lives, these same people may be oblivious to malware running in the background. They don't know that they may have viruses infecting their hard drives. The act of forgiveness is something that every human being must do if they want to be happy.

Pause for a moment to ask yourself if you identify with any of the players in the political melodrama above. Think about what character best matches your value system and espouses your point of view. Which of these combatants would openly confess that they need a dose of forgiveness? Probably no one would. Donald Trump needs forgiveness for seeking retaliation, not reconciliation. Bill O'Reilly needs forgiveness for the cheap tricks he used in trying to belittle candidate Trump in front of the television cameras. Megyn Kelly needs forgiveness for using her position as a debate moderator to advance her own agenda. While her question may have been a fair one, she asked it in a way that was sure to humiliate the candidate. *Fox News* didn't have to cave in to political correctness to do the right thing, so the network shares some of the responsibility for what happened.

When we are hurt (when we allow ourselves to be hurt) our natural defenses take over. You may have your own version of these: "How dare that woman talk to me that way?"; "That guy's a real son-of-a-bitch. He fired me so he could hire someone younger at half the salary."; or, "My husband always wants to control everything. He never listens to a word I say." Each of these statements implies that the problem rests with the "other guy." After all, you didn't say anything to merit that kind of tongue lashing; you were a good employee, who didn't deserve to be fired; you have tried a hundred times to show your husband that he is too overbearing. Why would another driver flip you off on the freeway? When Aunt Susie refuses to attend your son's wedding because of something that happened years ago, who is in the wrong? When you know you are drinking too much, what excuse do you give? All of these questions require transparency and vulnerability in seeking answers.

Brené Brown in *Daring Greatly* stresses the importance of being vulnerable in transforming "the way we live, love, parent, and lead." Brown draws an important distinction between shame and guilt, two primitive and pervasive human emotions. When we are feeling guilty, we say to ourselves, "I have done something bad." When we feel shame we tell ourselves, "I *am* bad."[9] We see guilt as a misdemeanor, while being ashamed of ourselves is a capital offense. Our experience suggests that when a person feels shame they tend to withdraw, avoiding the reality of negative things that happen. A person who feels guilty, on the other hand, is more likely to admit to wrongdoing and offer an apology. When someone makes a rude gesture toward you, it may be because they are angry at someone else and have chosen you as a convenient target. It is also possible that you did something to precipitate the rude response, in which case you are guilty for complicity in the episode. In this latter instance, it is best to admit your error, ask God for forgiveness and move on.

Aunt Susie might be holding a grudge and trying to shame you for being a "bad person." If you choose to take on (become burdened by) this shame, you could easily slip into the quicksand of self-hatred. It is plausible that you too are part of the problem, which falls into the category of "unfinished business." The best way to handle this situation is to recognize your

---

[9] Brené Brown, *Daring Greatly, How the Courage to Be Vulnerable Transforms the Way We Live, Love, Parent, and Lead* (New York: Gotham Books, 2012), 71.

role, empathize with Aunt Susie's anguish and try to reconcile your differences. The straightforward, apologetic approach is the proven way to go.

A potentially deadly circumstance arises when you are in denial of actions that are clearly wrong. Substance abuse and other addictions are ways of coping with life that always lead to serious erosion of your sense of self-worth. When you begin to make excuses for these behaviors, you dig yourself in deeper. The only way out of the dark night of addiction is with the helping hands of other human beings. Recovery starts when you are honest enough to admit your helplessness before God and everybody (Refer back to the Twelve Steps of A.A., beginning on page 41.). Whenever you are embroiled in a drama, it is best to start with yourself in looking for the source of the problem.

Self-examination requires a mindset of vulnerability, the willingness to take a risk—the kind of risk that leads you to be the first one to say, "I love you," after an argument, or causes you to invest in a relationship, not knowing whether or not it will work out. Vulnerability is the spawning ground for joy, love, creativity and a sense of belonging. When we practice being vulnerable, we will find that we are God's unique and beautiful creation, and that we don't have to pretend to be someone else.

Paradox of insight

I find the word "insight" to be one of the more misleading words in the English language. Insight is usually thought of as an "Aha!" experience, when we discover something new and unexpected. It's great when we expand our knowledge through external sources, but insight is a paradoxical word. "In-sight" is really "sight-in," that is, the view we get of the inside, not necessarily the other way around.

Here's an example of what we call the *paradox of insight*. When I look out my living room window, I sometimes see people walking by my neighbor Steve's yard and helping themselves to the fruit on his lemon tree. Now, this tree is usually filled with juicy lemons, and being right next to the street, it's tempting to passersby. Steve even placed a bunch of lemons in a box with a "free" sign on it, and someone took everything, box included. It bothers me when I see these "thieves" in action, but thus far I have restrained myself and have yet to do much about the situation, except to remain frustrated; adding one more condition to my happiness. Several times, as I hurried to the front door to reproach a lemon thief, my wife yelled, "Stop." Each time, I wisely stopped.

As I continued to stew about this, I made several observations. First, human beings can't pass up a "freebee," and the lemons are just begging to be picked. Second, the tree has a bumper crop and there have been years when Steve couldn't give them away fast enough. Next, the thieves are, after all, our neighbors. Lastly, the problem is Steve's, not mine. These insights were helpful, but the really insightful part of this story came when I examined my motives and tried to understand why this situation aggravates me so much. The act of taking another's property is morally wrong, a violation of my values. Alerting Steve to what is happening is appropriate for me to do. So far, so good. But, do I really think I could I have said anything to the thieves that they don't already know? Would I feel better if I unleashed my anger on my neighbors? Would it have been worth it to have my wife angry with me for precipitating a confrontation in our front yard? The answer to all of these questions is easy. . . no!

As I have grown older, I have learned that I tend to want to be in control. This is an especially bad habit in circumstances that should be outside my scope of concern. Once I told Steve what I observed, I needed to step away and let him handle it. There are other ways to make the point and hopefully the lemon thieves will ask next time. I still hold them accountable for their wrongdoing, but since I gained an understanding of my motivations, I feel much better about my involvement. If you want to draw a clear picture of what's going on in your life, turn your vision inward; get underneath your own skin. In the great lemon caper, it first appeared that the only solution was to bring the thieves to justice. But in the paradox of insight, I learned that I owned a piece of the problem. I had attached myself to getting an outcome consistent with my standards of right and wrong. Insight came, not from the *outside in*, but from the *inside out*.

The enemy is us

As we stated in the Introduction, there is nothing particularly original in this book. We gratefully stand on the shoulders of those who have already covered the territory, like pioneering psychiatrist Carl Jung, who made this disquieting observation about self-examination:

> The acceptance of oneself is the essence of the whole moral problem and the epitome of a whole outlook on life. That I feed the hungry, that I forgive an insult, that I love my enemy in the name of Christ—all these are undoubtedly great virtues. What I do unto the least of my brethren, that I do unto Christ. But what if I should discover that the least among them all, the poorest of all the beggars, the most impudent of all the offenders, the very enemy himself—that these are within me, and that I

myself stand in need of the alms of my own kindness—that I myself am the enemy who must be loved—what then?. . . We hide it from the world; we refuse to admit ever having met this least among the lowly in ourselves.[10]

Self-acceptance is the "epitome of a whole outlook on life." When a man finally sees that he is the "most impudent of all the offenders," he stands in need of forgiveness. Once he accepts who he is (has a vision of his True Self) with all his human foibles, then all that is left to do is to forgive himself. This radical acceptance of self is the entry point for letting go. It is by all accounts a grief experience; a part of a man must die before his new life can spring forth.

For Earth Day 1971, cartoonist Walt Kelly featured Pogo and his pal Porkypine stumbling through a swamp littered with garbage and debris. Porkypine says, "Ah, Pogo, the beauty of the forest primeval gets me in the heart." Pogo sarcastically replies, "It gets *me* in the *feet*, Porkypine." As they stop to survey the wretched scene before them, Porkypine concedes, "It *is* hard walkin' on this stuff." Pogo then utters this now famous aphorism: "Yep, son, we have met the enemy, and he is us."[11]

Here are five questions to ask yourself to gain insight into your own need for forgiveness:

1. How would you describe your relationship with your father? Your mother?

2. Is there anything they could have done differently to make your life better?

---

[10] *Goodreads*, http://www.goodreads.com/quotes/230446-the-acceptance-of-oneself-is-the-essence-of-the-whole, (September 15, 2016).

[11] *Yahoo*, http://www.bing.com/images/search?q=pogo+cartoon+enemy&qpvt=pogo+cartoon+enemy&qpvt=pogo+ccartoo+enemy&qpvt=pogo+cartoon+enemy&FORM=IGRE, (September 9, 2016).

3. If you could change one thing about your spouse/significant other, what would that be?

4. Has someone you care about tried to hurt you and not earnestly apologized?

5. Has something happened to you that has caused you to feel like a victim?

Make a written response to the five questions above. We will consider your answers later in the book.

4

MESSENGER IN BLUE

"It is one of the most beautiful compensations of this life that no man can sincerely try to help another without helping himself."
RALPH WALDO EMERSON

"Linda Martinez" was an elementary school teacher for many years. One day, a letter arrived from one of her former students. After reading it, she said to her husband, "Wow! You should look at this." The student had written, "Dear Mrs. Martinez, when I was in your third-grade class, I stole things from you. I would go through your desk and your purse and take cash and other things like pens or gum. I have been living with this a long time, and I want to tell you I'm sorry." Linda recalled that this woman had been one of her pupils some twenty years before. Enclosed with the letter was a hundred dollar gift certificate to a fancy department store. To compensate for what she had taken, she asked that Linda accept the gift certificate and buy something nice for herself. Linda was at choice. She could have chosen to be angry, but instead her unqualified reaction was to forgive her former student and accept the peace offering. Her husband "Robert" reacted quite differently when he saw the letter and his response was not so conciliatory. He felt that the woman was a thief and was just looking to feel better by buying Linda off. Although it had happened decades earlier, Robert was incensed that someone would take advantage of his wife like that. He was in favor of returning the gift certificate as soon as possible. Fortunately, Linda didn't listen to him and she happily went shopping, courtesy of the repentant woman.

What Robert later realized was that his ill feelings toward the woman were coming from his own projections about himself. The woman's letter conjured up all the dark shadows he had in his own past. He too had been a thief, but unlike the woman, had yet to exorcise his personal demons. He didn't have a grudge with her at all; he was angry at himself. Perhaps, without knowing it, he envied the woman's courage. But, by her demonstration of compassion and understanding, Linda showed Robert a better way.

This episode illustrates the beauty of forgiveness. The woman had made a forthright self-examination and admitted her guilt (the act of self-forgiveness), then sought to make amends. She asked for forgiveness in her honorable letter and she made material restitution for what she had stolen. Linda acknowledged her honesty, forgave her and let it go. The student and her teacher are all square and the universe is in better balance.

This woman must have suffered deeply during the long period of her unforgiven-ness, but now she has paid her debt and moved on. For his part, Robert is truly sorry that he showed so little empathy. It's not likely to happen, but should their paths ever cross, he intends to tell her how much he admires her courage and integrity.

Victims and offenders

In any forgiveness story, it is essential to have clarity about who should be considered a victim and who should not. A victim is someone who "is acted on and usually adversely affected by a force or agent; that is subjected to oppression, hardship, or mistreatment."[1] Clearly, there are real victims in this world, who have no control over circumstances and events that negatively impact them. Random acts of violence, parental abuse and human trafficking are sad examples of happenings that do damage to millions of blameless people. Victims of such crimes have done nothing to invite these reprehensible actions by perpetrators who exert power over them. Conversely, we need to carefully examine the motives of people who make dubious claims about being victimized. This should not be thought of as "victim blaming," but as an honest attempt to get to the crux of who has been injured and who should be asking for forgiveness and making amends. Choice is always the operative word in a given situation. No one wishes or chooses to be a victim, but *victimhood* is a choice that some people make because it gives them license to blame someone else for creating their problems. They hope that the "offender" will feel guilty enough to pay for the damage that was inflicted. Although this sort of "victim" claims no personal culpability, he is "living a lie" and his charade becomes destructive to the human family. Unfortunately, victimhood has become a style of life for some people.

The Drama Triangle© is a model of social interaction that was conceived by Stephen Karpman, M.D. to illustrate the detrimental impact of unresolved conflict.[2] In Karpman's model (Figure 2, page 74) there

---

[1] *Merriam-Webster* online dictionary.
[2] *Yahoo*, https://www.karpmandramatriangle.com/; https://en.

are three life-positions that a person can take: Persecutor, Victim and Rescuer. The Persecutor is the "bad guy," who is responsible for causing pain and suffering to the Victim. The Victim can feel helpless and hopelessly trapped. When the Rescuer (by invitation, or not) comes to the Victim's aid, everyone is led right into a "triad of doom."

Karpman Drama Triangle©

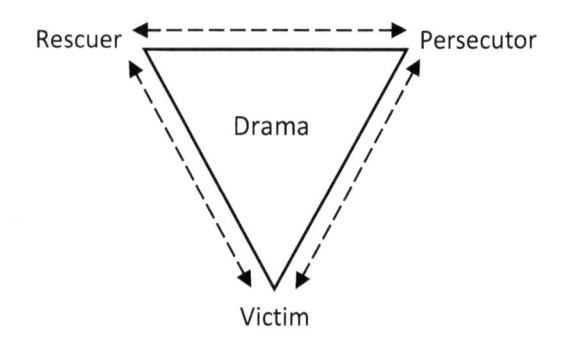

Rescuer ←--------→ Persecutor

Drama

Victim

Figure 2

The Rescuer, often beset by his own conscious or unconscious feelings of guilt and remorse, enters the fray with good intentions, but as we shall see, he errs in doing so.

In order to get their psychological needs met, the "Triangle Players" may intensify and even shift roles as the drama unfolds. The Victim can turn the tables on his oppressor and become the Persecutor himself. Meanwhile, the Rescuer can become the target of Persecutor #1 and claim to be a victim, as well. It is all very complicated, especially as it gets more and more difficult to decipher who is who in this trio of dramatic actors.

---

wikipedia.org/wiki/Karpman_drama_triangle/, (November 29, 2017).

In *Beyond Drama*, Dr. Nate Regier and Jeff King make the following insightful observation:

> Drama is what happens when people struggle against themselves or others to feel justified about the things they do to gain negative attention, with or without awareness. Drama is an energy vampire, sucking the lifeblood of everyone and everything around it. Drama strains relationships, sidelines teams, and causes companies to operate at a fraction of their capacity. Drama is amazingly predictable yet incredibly resistant to change.[3]

Let's look at a simple example of how the Drama Triangle works in "sucking the lifeblood out of everyone." In tears, little brother Bobby runs to his father and says, "Johnny just threw a skate at me." The stage is now set with Bobby cast in the role of Victim, Johnny as Persecutor and Dad as Rescuer. What does Bobby want his father to do? What should he do? In effect, Bobby is saying, "Please rescue me and punish Johnny." Suppose Dad reacts angrily and says to Johnny, "What are you doing, throwing a roller skate at your little brother?" A predictable response is, "Bobby started it. He hit me with a baseball." The players have just exchanged roles (life-positions) with Johnny auditioning as Victim and Bobby cast as Persecutor. What does Dad do now? This is one of those times when a parent needs to exercise caution. Dad does not want to come to either victim's rescue and he

---

[3] Nate Regier and Jeff King, *Beyond Drama, Transcending Energy Vampires* (Newton, KS: Next Element Pub., 2013), from the Overview. Note: If you want to visualize the effects of the Drama Triangle©, compare Figure 2 with Figure 1a on page 46. When you are in healthy, happy relationships, stress is manageable. But when drama happens, the triangle inverts and all the "bad stuff" flows downhill, pushing the victim toward distress.

does not want to end up "abandoning" them either. *The goal when invited into the drama triangle is not to rescue and not abandon the players who are in conflict.* If Dad says, "Boys, you will have to figure this out on your own. Don't expect me to solve your problems for you," this would be taken by both boys as a form of abandonment. If this were to happen, what are the odds that Bobby and Johnny will work it out themselves? It is far more likely that they will feel rejected by their father and then go to their mother in search of another potential rescuer. So, the game of life goes on! When it comes to resolving conflict, the Drama Triangle might as well be the Bermuda Triangle. You are lucky if you come out unscathed.[4]

The win-lose strategy of the players in the Drama Triangle invariably leads to lose-lose. In choosing to perpetuate victimhood, people will almost certainly lose self-esteem, risk damaging key relationships and diminish their capacity to influence others. The victim will finally begin to crawl out of the swamp when he is motivated enough to seek what he really wants—love, happiness, connection and personal significance. When roles are reversed and the victim elects to become the persecutor, he also needs forgiveness. The spell of the Drama Triangle is broken when one of the players can say to himself, "I am undeserving, but I refuse to play the victim." This admission is a monumental move toward the grace of forgiveness.

If this example seems simplistic, consider how the Drama Triangle works on a much bigger stage. On August 9, 2014 in Ferguson, Missouri, a deadly altercation took place between a black man and a white police officer. According to police, eighteen-year old Michael Brown was believed to be a suspect in a

---

[4] We have deliberately left out the "best scenario" for resolving this family's dispute. Our purpose is to point out the poor choices a person can make when engaged in conflict. How would you solve this dilemma?

holdup of a nearby convenience store. When confronted, Brown got into a scuffle with Officer Darren Wilson and fled the scene on foot. He was pursued by the officer and fatally shot. Eyewitnesses offered conflicting accounts of what happened, and when the Grand Jury did not find sufficient evidence to indict Officer Wilson for Brown's death, violence erupted in cities across the nation. In Ferguson, rioting and looting accounted for millions of dollars in damage and brought racial tensions to the boiling point. Local authorities appealed for help and Federal troops were brought in to quell the violence and keep the peace. President Barack Obama weighed in on the controversy when he said that black citizens had a legitimate right to be angry at their treatment by police. Citing a Justice Department report on the Ferguson Police Department, he said, "What had been happening in Ferguson was oppressive and objectionable and was worthy of protest." He further noted that "structures of racism" were found in Ferguson and exist in many other places across the country.[5]

It is immaterial whether or not the President's statement was accurate. When he intervened, he took sides and became the Rescuer. This single statement by the President of the United States, elected to represent *all* Americans, probably did more harm to race relations than anything that happened in Ferguson. The struggle against the evil of racism is a righteous and a worthy undertaking, and it would be best if our president was America's leading voice for action and reconciliation. But this time he chose the wrong means of dissent. While he may have shored up support among certain constituencies, he was perceived by many to have abandoned law enforcement. In

---

[5] Michael D. Shear, *New York Times*, "Obama Discusses Ferguson with Jimmy Kimmel," https://www.nytimes.com/2015/03/13/us/politics/obama-discusses-ferguson-with-jimmy-kimmel.html, (March 12, 2015).

acting as both Rescuer and Persecutor, he perpetuated the Drama Triangle and nothing he did helped to bring a divided nation closer together.

President Obama violated a cardinal rule of conflict resolution. But suppose he had taken this position in the immediate aftermath of the tragedy in Ferguson: "Let's be clear, the events that occurred in Ferguson, Missouri are terribly hurtful and regrettable. We mourn the loss of Michael Brown and our hearts go out to his family. The looting and violence that occurred in response to the Grand Jury's decision was also regrettable. But do we Americans have to continue to act this way in resolving our differences? I ask my fellow citizens, 'How can we work together to escape the cycle of blame we find ourselves in?' People on all sides have deep feelings and these feelings need to be expressed and listened to, so that there will never be another scene like the one we witnessed in Ferguson. Nothing good will come from pointing the finger and casting blame on 'the other guy.' Nothing of lasting worth will come from calling yourself a 'victim' and advocating violence as a response. Nothing positive will be achieved by blaming Michael Brown or the Grand Jury. The worst thing that can happen is for good people to simply bury their heads in the sand and ignore what is happening. While it may be impossible to know every detail of the events that night in Ferguson, we do know one thing. A young man lost his life and we can honor his memory, not with bitterness and retribution, but by accepting the fact that our country has a big problem. The solution will be found only after we acknowledge our brother's feelings and engage in an honest dialogue about what separates us. Healing our wounds and strengthening our nation will be achieved, not in fear and with enmity, but through love and compassion." In crisis times, it is not enough to tell the obvious truth. People in positions of power and influence are called to speak to a deeper, more fundamental truth.

Anything we do that does not bring us together serves to divide us. There is no neutral when people are deeply split on issues that affect us all, like racial inequality, gay marriage, immigration, climate change . . . you name it! When we continue to foster division and alienation, we suppress the necessary conditions for forgiveness and reconciliation. Who will make the first big move in reaching across the divide, not with a clenched fist, but with an open hand? In Chapter Seven we will suggest an alternative approach as we seek answers to the systemic problems of racism and divisiveness.

Forgiveness scenarios

When it comes to forgiveness, here are four possible scenarios that are commonplace, inescapable consequences of everyday existence:

A. You are the offender. You have done something that requires another person's forgiveness.

B. You are the victim and the offender asks for your forgiveness.

C. You are the victim, but the offender is unrepentant or unavailable.

D. You are both victim and offender.[6]

The first two scenarios are fairly straightforward, whereas the others can get complicated. In C, you may have been victimized by someone you don't know. If it was a criminal offense such as burglary or rape, the

---

[6] While these are the most common ones, there may be other scenarios that merit consideration. For example, when the Rescuer in the Drama Triangle becomes the Persecutor (offender).

perpetrator is unlikely to return to apologize. In the last scenario, it may be impossible to determine who did what to whom, and when. In a long standing marital dispute, for example, emotions run so high that no one remembers who started it in the first place. It degenerates into "attack and defend" combat, where even honest commentary is perceived as a personal affront. Then, there are times when you come to the place of forgiveness, but the other person is unavailable. What do you do then?

Late one December, I received a letter from a young man named John. I first met him through my son-in-law, who invited John to join us at our cottage in the lake country of northern Ontario. The cottage is isolated in the midst of a spectacular wilderness, the perfect place to escape from the frenetic pace of city life and enjoy the pleasures of the natural world. In one of our conversations, I shared with John my journey to forgiveness with my father and how much happier I was because of it. I don't remember that he made a specific response, but he seemed to be engaged with my story. Here is what John wrote in his letter:

> I never got a chance to give you a special thanks. I think it was two years ago you were talking about forgiveness and the last step is to ask the other person to forgive you. I was so hung up on trying to forgive my father (me-centered) that I couldn't move forward from the grudges I held. Once I realized that I owned some of the pain between us, I was able to truly reconcile with him. Now, he has been dead since 2000, but in my prayers I can talk to him and I feel all is well now. Whatever was between us has been healed.

John's letter was one of the best Christmas presents I have ever received. When I finished reading it, I just sat there for a long time. I was so grateful, knowing that one more person had discovered the key to letting go and finding peace. When I called John to thank him for his letter, he explained how good he felt about it, but that it is a different feeling when you have to forgive someone who is gone. In his moments of silence, in the place of his solitude, John reached out and asked his dad for forgiveness. He received the response he had been praying for. John has graciously allowed me to share his intimate letter with others who might benefit from his story. This is how you forgive someone *in absentia*. Let the Spirit be your guide. Just say the words and all will be well.

Let's consider the first scenario. You may be unaware that you offended a co-worker by a casual comment you made at the water cooler. In the interests of getting along in the workplace, your co-worker disguised her negative reaction. (Remember, more harm is done by people who take offense than by those who give offense.) Assuming she doesn't approach you about it afterwards and you don't pick up on it by a change in her behavior, an apology is not called for. But suppose she confides in one of your office buddies, who in turn gives you a heads up that something is wrong. Then, that's a horse of a different color. Although you may have had no ill intentions, your words were taken wrong and you should do something about it. A good approach is to say to her, "I thought about our conversation on Tuesday and I realize I said something to offend you. I'm sorry. I like working with you and hope that you will accept my apology." Once you earnestly apologize, the ball is in her court. She can choose to forgive you, or not. If she can't let it go, she will remain mired in the mud of her afflictive emotions. There won't be reconciliation between you until she unconditionally accepts your apology. In either case, you are genuinely sorry and you have made amends, so you are off the hook. She can get *her hooks* out by accepting your apology and moving on.[7]

What if there had been an ongoing feud between you and your co-worker leading up to the water cooler incident. Now, that changes things. In this case, you both had ill intentions, so therefore each of you qualifies as both victim and offender (Scenario D). Who will make the first move, here? Let's assume you think about it and realize that you have been wrong to prolong the pettiness. You might approach her and say, "I don't want our disagreement to go any further. I realize that I have said some mean things to hurt you. Please forgive me. In the interests of being completely honest, I must tell you that I too have been hurt by some of the things you said to me. I hope that we can figure this out." Once again, your co-worker can choose forgiveness, or not. She might tell you that she forgives you, while still failing to accept full responsibility for her own actions. Here again, you get your hooks out and regain your personal equilibrium, while she remains stuck. Hopefully, she reciprocates and asks you to forgive her, too. You easily accept her apology and the office is a happier place.

One afternoon, I was hurrying to make a purchase at one of the giant warehouse stores. As I walked in the direction of a jovial looking representative from a satellite dish company, I knew he was preparing to give me his spiel. But before he could get a word out, I cut him off. I had just changed cable providers and I knew what he was about to say. "No thanks," I facetiously said, "I love seeing all those cable wires behind my TV." The guy looked at me like he had just seen a real idiot. I felt badly, but not enough to

---

[7] We use the word "hooks" to refer to pain and suffering that we bring on ourselves when we choose (consciously, or not) to allow events to dominate our behavior, and thus restrict our happiness. The barbs of the hook hold fast until we face the truth and begin to accept our role in things that happened.

apologize, so I quickly paid my bill and left. For weeks, I couldn't get this incident out of my head. My remark was condescending and stupid. The salesman *had* seen an idiot! Every time I was in the store after that, I looked for him, but without success. Then, months later, there he was, standing in the very same spot where we met before. This time I let him finish his sales pitch and we started a conversation. I said, "A while back, I was rude to you and I'm sorry." He said, "I remember you now, yeah. . . no problem." We both laughed and went our separate ways.

Most often, forgiveness stories involve people we know and care about, but I can't tell you how much better I felt for having made amends with someone I probably will never see again. Once I walked in the direction of my pain by admitting the naked truth of what I had done, my hooks began to loosen. Then, when I asked for forgiveness, they came free.

Where do acorns grow?

Ralph Waldo Emerson once said this about one of nature's underrated players, "The creation of a thousand forests is in one acorn."[8] A few years ago, I began carrying acorns around with me, as a reminder of their immense power. I almost never pass up an acorn on the trail without pausing to marvel at its humble simplicity. Sometimes, I pick up the nicer ones and drop them into my pocket for good luck. For me, the acorn is more than just an example of the little guy who does big things; the acorn is my symbol for forgiveness and reconciliation.

WisdomGuides© supports a regional not-for-profit organization that has been around for many years and

---

[8] *Brainyquote*, http://www.brainyquote.com/quotes/keywords/acorn.html, (January 30, 2016).

serves hundreds of needy families in the community. It is fairly typical of non-profits in that it is governed by a board of trustees who report to a regional director. The stakeholders are local citizens who sustain the organization not only financially, but with their time and talents as well. These people exercise a strong voice in the way the organization conducts business and hires its senior management.

Some years ago, the CEO suddenly resigned and moved away. While the search for a successor was underway, the organization was being run by the board of trustees. The board hired a promising candidate to perform interim duties and be evaluated for a longer term assignment. There were some stakeholders who felt manipulated by the board in what was perceived as a less than transparent selection process. However, the candidate had impeccable academic credentials and was an excellent speaker, so there was hope that he might prove to be a good choice.

There were several unresolved issues surrounding the former CEO's departure and the community had become deeply divided between his staunch supporters and those who wanted a change of course. Before the interim CEO had even unpacked his bags, he was already under heavy scrutiny.

About this time, Tom and I were elected to serve three-year terms on the board of trustees. Tom had previously been in a top leadership position and it was my second stint on the board. We hoped we could fairly represent the interests of the entire community, especially those who felt disenfranchised by the direction that was being taken. And we prayed that our corporate consulting experience would be helpful to the incoming CEO in leading a large, multi-faceted not-for-profit corporation.

It was apparent that our new CEO had a very specific agenda that he intended to roll out as quickly as he could. The key leaders and active sustainers of the organization were older, upper middle class whites, which was not reflective of the demographic of the community being served. In his efforts to broaden ethnic membership, the new CEO made a number of personnel moves that rankled a large segment of the constituency. Several longtime employees were released and the director of education was demoted. A popular staff member with duties at the organization's food bank was reassigned. The murmur of discontent became louder when it was noticed that, while all the affected staff members were white, their replacements were almost unanimously people of color. The CEO made a number of "house calls" to introduce himself to key stakeholders, and in several conversations he inquired about racist attitudes within the community. With distrust already festering, he invited the issue of race to subtly creep into the picture.

As the CEO consolidated his leadership base with the executive committee of the board of trustees, the division widened. The board was split on almost every key initiative and policy, becoming largely dysfunctional and ineffective. The situation degraded into a caustic game of attack and defend, where both sides dug themselves deeper and deeper into defensive positions. Hoping to get the board in a better frame of mind, the CEO scheduled a board retreat in Santa Barbara, California. During the three-hour trip along the coast, Tom and I strategized on how we could douse the conflagration.

Our hearts were heavy when we arrived at the retreat center in the afternoon on day one. We bunked together in a miniature room that must have been built from blueprints for a prison cell, but we did have privacy. So, we closed the door and reviewed our plans for the first meeting. When the board convened, each member was asked to make a statement. Comments ran the gamut between hopefulness and unhappiness, but no one addressed the elephant in the room until it came around to Tom. He gave a full, behind the scenes account of how he and several others had been activists in the departure of the former CEO and he openly accepted his share of the blame for the mess we were in. He humbly made this confession, "I am sorry for what I did. I should have done things differently. I need your forgiveness."

His words of contrition didn't get the conciliatory response we hoped it would, so when it was my turn to speak I praised Tom for his honesty and tried to get the board to recognize what he had just done. But my efforts at reconciliation also fell on deaf ears and I had that terrible, empty feeling you get when you run out of options and don't know where to turn. After what seemed like a long time, the CEO finally called for a timeout. Tom and I walked up the road, where we found a bench and sat down under a shady oak tree. He began our conversation with, "Well, that didn't go so well, did it?" What an understatement that was! Then, as we looked out over the grounds, something astonishing happened. A blue jay landed right at our feet and picked up an acorn that was lying on the ground. Unperturbed by our presence, he promptly flew into the tree and lit on a branch that was just inches above our heads. Now, I don't know how much you know about jays, but this is not their normal behavior. They are wily birds who usually give humans a wide berth. We remained perfectly still as we watched the bird crack open the acorn and devour its contents. Then, after a couple of minutes, it flexed its wings and flew away. We looked dumbfounded at each other and instinctively we knew. . . "It was Grace," said Tom. The element of the unexpected is one of Nature's techniques for making her point. I have had things like this happen to me before, but that's the closest I have ever come to a blue jay. I was grateful that in the midst of my tribulation I got a glimpse of something pure and beautiful. Our impasse with the board remained unresolved and not much of any consequence was accomplished at the retreat.

Back home, emotions were running higher than a kite in a windstorm, where trustee meetings often degraded into *ad hominem* assaults between warring factions. This sort of thing doesn't belong in such a setting, but it became the order of the day. Every new proposal, every personnel move and budget line item was viewed with suspicion by half the stakeholders. Meetings of the trustees that would normally have but a handful of people in attendance drew standing room only crowds. Things took an even sharper turn into the muck when supporters' names were published alongside the financial contributions they had made to the organization. The place had become a tinderbox.

The regional director showed no signs of stepping in, so a group calling itself "Concerned Citizens" began circulating a petition and holding meetings to garner support for a full-fledged mutiny. Meanwhile, the executive committee of the board continued to meet in secret with the CEO to strategize about what to do next. When the Concerned Citizens called for a community-wide meeting to present their takeover plans, the regional director finally intervened. Asserting his legal prerogatives, he halted the proceedings and assumed control of the corporation. The director then mandated that all board members attend a retreat, which he would lead. Prior to the retreat, he contacted me and persuaded me to represent the community as a special liaison to the board. Although I had been an active agent within the Concerned Citizens faction, I now had to shift gears and fairly represent the entire membership. That required me to take a different view of things by gaining insight into opposing positions.

The regional director hired a professional mediator to facilitate meetings at the retreat. In the first session, he recognized Tom as an expert in conflict resolution and I felt a glimmer of optimism when the two of them met in private to discuss what was really going on and consider what to do about it. During the morning of the final day, the mediator openly admitted that he had come to the retreat with very low expectations, but now felt that some progress was attainable. He made a point of sitting with me at lunch and alerted me that he would be calling on me at the start of the afternoon session. The session began with a moment of silence and when I bowed my head I noticed an acorn lying under my chair. Now, mind you, we were inside a building and there weren't any trees growing in the meeting room. I instinctively picked up the shiny little seed and placed it in my pocket. After a few opening remarks, the mediator said, "I want Ed to frame up what the problem is." It was obvious that this was my final chance at making a difference in the protracted stalemate. The stage was set for my moment of truth. I pulled the acorn from my pocket and held it hidden in my fist. As I searched for just the right words, I glanced out the window and saw a splendid California oak tree spread out against the rolling hills. Then it hit me! Words began gushing forth from deep in my soul. "There was once a magnificent oak tree in the forest. It was old and needed the arborist's attention, but it was very beautiful," I said. Then, opening my hand and displaying the acorn, I continued, "This acorn I'm holding represents the CEO's vision. It is a worthy vision, but there is a problem." I turned to the CEO, who was seated immediately to my right, and looking straight into his eyes, I said, "You cut down the beautiful oak tree to plant an acorn in its place. What you should have done is prune the tree and plant the acorn in the fertile soil surrounding it. Then both could grow. This is what happened to our wonderful organization. It is so sad." When I again looked toward the source of my inspiration, what do you suppose I saw? It may have been a blue jay, I am not sure. But, something was there. By now, I was utterly spent with emotion and tears were pouring down my cheeks. Everything was profoundly quiet and peaceful. When I surveyed the room, I saw that a miraculous shift had taken place. The look on the faces of the board members told that at last they were ready to start letting go. They had had enough!

Led by the facilitator, just about everyone began moving toward forgiveness. I led off by saying to the board chairperson, who had been one of my chief protagonists, "'Thomas', I am sorry for things I did and said to hurt you. Please forgive me." He said the same in return. I walked over to him and we embraced. I said, "I love you, Thomas." He said, "I love you, too." The people in the room that day made peace with one another, with the notable exception of the CEO. Regrettably, he could only admit, "I should have worked harder." Not long afterwards he relinquished his post, and after receiving a handsome severance package, he packed up and left town. To this day he has not reconciled with the people who were once under his care.

As their special representative on the board, there was something I needed to say to the community in order to get closure on the affair. At a public forum I made an apology for the board's lapses in judgment and failed leadership. I told my friends and neighbors that I knew many of them had been hurt and I asked them to find forgiveness in their hearts. After the meeting, several people who had been on the other side of the controversy offered words of appreciation and expressed their willingness to try to move on. The healing had begun, but the conflict had taken a heavy toll on the organization. In less than two years, nearly half its sustainers withdrew their financial support. Its reputation in the community took a big hit and the rumor was that it was no longer a welcoming place.

Another page was added to this story a few months later when three prominent members of the board of trustees made an appointment to meet with the regional director. Although he disavowed any responsibility, it was widely felt that the director had not acted in the best interests of the local community. He knew "Rome was burning," but waited far too long to put the fire out and the results were devastating. The purpose of the meeting was to confront him and urge him to issue a public apology for not acting sooner. He was surprised and took it as an insult that anyone had the hutzpah to accuse him of wrongdoing. His disingenuous response was, "I will have to think about it." Whether he thought about it or not is unknown, because afterwards he avoided his accusers and never offered to mend fences.

A number of years have now passed and our wounds have been healed. We have a much smaller organization now, but at least we are happy working together and making a difference. Who knows where we would be today if we had continued down the road we were on.[9]

Now that you know the whole story, you shouldn't wonder why I pick up acorns along the trail, or why I keep such a sharp eye out for flickers of blue among the trees.

> *Next time you walk under an oak tree, pick up an acorn and ask yourself, "Whom do I need to forgive?"*

---

[9] We have used fictitious names in this story, but these events actually occurred as told. This is a prime example of how forgiveness works to unite groups of people who passionately believe that their side is "in the right."

5

FEEDING OF WOLVES

"The bitterest tears shed over graves are for words left unsaid and deeds left undone."
HARRIET BEECHER STOWE

A wise old Cherokee once told this story to his grandson, who came to him with anger at a friend who had done him an injustice:

> I too, at times, have felt a great hate for those that have taken so much, with no sorrow for what they do. But hate wears you down, and does not hurt your enemy. It is like taking poison and wishing your enemy would die. I have struggled with these feelings many times. It is as if there were two wolves inside me. One is good and does no harm. He lives in harmony with all around him, and does not take offense when no offense was intended. He will only fight when it is right to do so, and in the right way. But the other wolf, ah! He is full of anger. The littlest thing will set him into a fit of temper. He fights everyone, all the time, for no

reason. He cannot think because his anger and hate are so great. It is helpless anger, for his anger will change nothing. Sometimes it is hard to live with these wolves inside me, for both of them try to dominate my spirit.[1]

The boy looked intently into his grandfather's eyes and asked, "Which one wins, Grandfather?" The old man smiled and said, "The one I feed."

In the first chapter, we looked at the afflictive emotions and what they can do to us if left unchecked. Human beings live with two wolves inside them. One is the wolf of enmity and bitterness, while the other is the wolf of compassion and forgiveness. We feed the wolves by the choices we make. Which wolf do you feed?

Forgiving your father

Here is another gem from the *WisdomGuides©* book of wit and wisdom: "If you keep doing what you're doing, you'll keep getting what you're getting." If you choose to remain in a fractured relationship with someone who matters to you, you will keep feeding the wolf that is eating you up inside. Until one of you breaks the stalemate by doing something radical, the situation will remain ugly.

Recently, I asked my friend Michael, "Do you know anything about forgiveness?" This is the kind of open ended question that can get all sorts of bizarre answers, unless of course, the person knows exactly what you are asking. Michael's immediate response was, "I know a lot about forgiveness. I know that my

---

[1] First People webpage, http://www.firstpeople.us/FP-Html-Legends/Two Wolves-Cherokee.html, (February 4, 2016).

father used to beat the crap out of me all the time, and now I call him every day and tell him that I love him."

How does a man forgive his father, who regularly beat him as though he were some kind of wild animal? How can the words, "I forgive you," come from the same lips that were silenced by the back of his father's hand? What does it take for a young man to face his Dad and tell him that he has released his wolf of bitterness, letting go of all judgment and condemnation? Surely, this takes more courage than most of us can muster.

There are other significant questions to think about. How can a father who has done these things to his own son ever forgive himself? And are there things the son has done that call for his father's forgiveness? A lot of things have to go right for a father and son to reconcile their differences.

In the Hermitage in Saint Petersburg, Russia hangs what is regarded by art critics as one of the greatest pictures ever painted. *The Return of the Prodigal Son* was one of the last works by Dutch master Rembrandt van Rijn (1606-69). The painting depicts a young man in tattered clothing on his knees, with his head resting plaintively against an old man's breast. The old man is bent over, his hands gently placed on the young man's shoulders. The look on his face is one of understanding and compassion, the look of one who is profoundly human.

Meanwhile, the scene is being viewed from the periphery by three other men. The faces of the old man and the most prominent onlooker are lighted in a way that immediately draws the eye. The old man is the father of both the kneeling man and the onlooker, his eldest son. The story had begun a few years earlier when the impetuous younger son asked for his share of his father's estate. After his request was granted, he promptly left for a faraway country where he led a life of debauchery and self-indulgence. When he was drained of his finances and his pride, he returned home to ask for his father's forgiveness.

Rembrandt's inspiration for the painting came from the Biblical parable of a runaway son. In this quintessential tale of mercy, Jesus tells of the young man's destitution.

> After he had spent everything, there was a severe famine in that whole country, and he began to be in need. So he went and hired himself out to a citizen of that country, who sent him to his fields to feed pigs. He longed to fill his stomach with the pods that the pigs were eating, but no one gave him anything. When he came to his senses, he said, "How many of my father's hired servants have food to spare, and here I am starving to death! I will set out and go back to my father and say to him: Father, I have sinned against heaven and against you. I am no longer worthy to be called your son; make me like one of your hired servants." So he got up and went to his father.[2]

This high-flying hotshot crash landed and found himself sitting in a pig sty, thoroughly stripped of all vestiges of his self-esteem. It was with great remorse and humility that he arrived at his father's house. The old man had been in deep distress, praying for his son's return. So, when he saw him in the distance he was jubilant and rushed to him, crying out, "This son of mine was dead and is alive again; he was lost and is found."[3] The prodigal, surprised to receive such a warm reception after what he had done, made a tearful confession and was unconditionally forgiven. Restored to stature in his father's house, the wayward one was

---

[2] Luke, 15: 14–20.
[3] Ibid., 15:24.

immediately dressed in fine clothes and a grand celebration was held in his honor.

The story could have ended there, but once again Jesus finds a way to get under your skin. A guy who squandered half his father's fortune is let off the hook and even rewarded with a big party. Give me a break! Who could blame big brother for resenting all the hoopla surrounding the bad boy's homecoming? The story continues:

> The older brother became angry and refused to go in. So his father went out and pleaded with him. But he answered his father, "Look! All these years I've been slaving for you and never disobeyed your orders. Yet you never gave me even a young goat so I could celebrate with my friends. But when this son of yours who has squandered your property with prostitutes comes home, you kill the fattened calf for him!"[4]

Rembrandt's skillful use of light dramatizes the elder son's seething emotions. He is immersed in what Henri Nouwen calls "the inner drama of the soul."[5]

There is an intriguing aspect of the painting that probably goes unnoticed by the casual observer. One would expect the prodigal and his father, the leading characters in the story, to be pictured in the center of the painting. They are not. Instead, Rembrandt places them on the left, while the elder son stands scornfully erect on the right. This juxtaposition is no accident. The artist clearly meant to portray the stark dichotomy between mercy and condemnation, between love and hatred. The distance separating them is the

---

[4] Ibid., 15:28–30
[5] Nouwen, *The Return of the Prodigal Son, A Story of Homecoming* (New York: Doubleday, 1992), 64. The authors are deeply grateful to Henri Nouwen for his moving insights into this archetypal parable of sin and redemption.

distance the unforgiver must travel to get to forgiveness; it is the wasteland between resentment and joyfulness. Unfortunately, for many of us a few inches on an artist's canvas is a journey too far.

When you look at the elder brother, do you see a vision of someone you know? Perhaps you see yourself. Were you the firstborn, for whom expectations were high? Were you the son or daughter who seldom strayed from the straight and narrow path—the one who lived by the rules and who didn't rock the boat because you wanted desperately to live up to your father's rigid expectations? Were you the son who watched as your father made compensations for your brother's shortcomings? Perhaps your father and brother grew closer together over the years, while you and your dad did not. Somewhere in your history, there was old business left unfinished, forgotten conflicts left unresolved. Then when he died, your father gave you a smaller inheritance than your siblings received. Perhaps you received no inheritance at all. You felt betrayed, as though your dad had lost faith in you, the good and loyal son.

My father died in 1998, and for several years afterwards I suffered through my own inner drama of the soul. For a time, the wolf of greed and envy held the upper hand. But I finally broke free and forgave my father for all his mistakes, for all the times he hurt me and never said, "I'm sorry." Like John in the previous chapter, I had to forgive him *in absentia*, but it worked all the same. I recognized that my father had done the best he knew, which often missed the mark. There were moments when I feel he misjudged me, but then I remember how proud he was to call me his son. I also had to come to terms with the part I owned in our sometimes difficult relationship, but I believe that my father has forgiven me, too. I am now at peace with the man who caused me more pain than anyone else in my life.

The summer before he died, we spent a few days together in Salmon, Idaho where he lived. We took several nostalgic driving trips through the beautiful Bitterroot Mountains and we talked a lot about our life together. We laughed and we cried and we reminisced. I think it was during these conversations that I began moving toward forgiven-ness, because more than ever before, I began to see his brokenness—his humanness. I told Dad I was grateful to him and would always remember the good times we had together. He was not able to reciprocate at the same level, but I am sure he understood what was happening between us.

There is something my father did that made it easier for me to forgive him after he was gone. It began in the early morning hours of April 21, 1994 at the border between Idaho and Montana. Dad and his fiancé were traveling a mountainous section of State Highway 93 that was under construction, when they collided head-on with a pilot truck. As a result of the violent impact, my father's lower leg had to be amputated, but Betty was not so lucky. She was pronounced dead while being transported by paramedic rescue to the hospital. When questioned, the operator of the truck maintained that Dad was driving on the wrong side of the road, which precipitated the accident. He was still in critical condition in a local hospital and was unable to give his version of the story until weeks later. As soon as he was well enough to communicate, investigators visited Dad in the hospital recovery unit. Yet unable to speak, he was given a pencil and paper, then asked several pertinent questions about what happened. Scribbling down just a few words at a time, he conveyed that he had been driving at the posted speed limit and was on his side of the highway when the collision occurred. Unlike the young woman who was driving the truck, my father had an enviable driving record. The case eventually ended up in a Missoula, Montana court-room. During the hearings, two independent investigators gave testimony that proved conclusively that the truck was going too fast for road conditions and veered into the oncoming lane of traffic, striking Dad's car. Under the weight of the overwhelming evidence, the truck driver broke down in tears and confessed that she had been lying. She admitted full responsibility for the accident and said she was deeply sorry for what happened. After the proceedings, as the parties were leaving the courthouse, my father did something that was truly extraordinary. He approached the broken woman, placed his hand on her shoulder and said: "You have been through a lot. I don't want you to carry this burden for the rest of your life. I forgive you!" The judge in the case awarded Dad a substantial sum of money, every penny of which he gave away to support people who needed it more than he did.

One thing my father didn't lack was courage. This story clearly shows that he was also gifted with the quality of compassion. His generosity became legend in the Salmon community, where he hosted a barbecue for the whole town when he first moved there. He met with the principal of the school and offered to purchase a new yellow bus for the students. When the police department declined his offer for a new radio car, he made a substantial contribution to the fire department. My father was a penitent man, too. Hobbled with his prosthetic leg, he would call his priest on the phone and arrange for a "drive by." Dad would pull up to the church, honk the horn and roll his window down. The priest would then give his best impersonation of a car hop, meeting him at the curb and hearing his confession. This unconventional method for receiving forgiveness happened more than once.

I took all these things into account and let go of all the negative feelings I had toward my father, once and for all. I cannot say for certain that he has forgiven me, but I sense that in our own way and in our own time we have finally "settled the score" with one another.

The father wound

Author John Eldridge is an activist in the battle for the spirit of masculinity. In *Wild at Heart,* Eldridge proposes that the great question every male asks himself is, "Am I good enough; am I powerful?" Until a man *knows* he is a man, he will "forever be trying to prove he is one."[6]

> The story of Adam's fall is every man's story. It is simple and straightforward, almost mythic in its brevity and depth. And so every man comes into the world set up for a loss of heart. Then comes the story we are much more aware of—our own story. Where Adam's story seems simple and straightforward, our own seems complex and detailed; many more characters are involved and the plot is sometimes hard to follow. But the outcome is always the same: a wound in the soul. Every boy, in his journey to become a man, takes an arrow in the center of his heart, in the place of his strength. Because the wound is rarely discussed and even more rarely healed, every man carries a wound. And the wound is nearly always given by his father.[7]

It is easy to see why this "wound" is rarely discussed. We are prone to run from anything that threatens our ego, things which might make us vulnerable. We dread knowing that we might not be the man we portray in real life, so we hide behind the chimera of our false self. And we men are not very good at cultivating intimate male friendships that allow for transparency

---

[6] John Eldridge, *Wild at Heart, Discovering the Secret of a Man's Soul* (New York: Thomas Nelson, 2001), 64.
[7] Ibid., 62.

and the sharing of our innermost thoughts and feelings.

The journey of a man's life is twofold: from boyhood to manhood and from manhood to old age. In the first part of the journey, as John Eldridge points out, a boy desperately needs to know if he is powerful enough, good enough to be called a man. If he gets affirmation from his father and other male role models, he will likely develop a healthy sense of his masculine self. This is why traditional male initiation rites have been so successful in preparing young men to assume the mantle of manhood. When a boy comes of age in a tribal society, he must undergo a series of steps before he is considered a full-fledged member of the clan. There is typically a bloodletting like circumcision, followed by his banishment into the wilderness. There, in solitude with his soul, the initiate must confront his demons and come face-to-face with the Great Spirit. This is a transformational experience, and when he returns to his village he is no longer a boy. The affirmation he receives from the elders establishes his position within the group and nurtures in him a strong, healthy ego structure. He learns to live and act according to time-honored customs, in ways that serve everyone in the tribe. Without the benefit of mature leadership, none of this could happen. Without a good mentor, a boy must try to discover for himself what it means to be a man.

One of the major problems we have today is that we no longer live in a society of elders, where boys are properly initiated into manhood by real men. Boys are too often "initiated" by *pseudo men*, males who look like men on the exterior, but who lack masculine integrity. The gang scene is a perfect illustration of what happens when *wisemen* are absent from boys' lives. Imagine what would happen in the tribal milieu if the initiate returned home and was told he didn't make the grade and didn't qualify for manhood. What would have happened if the prodigal son's father had rejected him instead of receiving him with love and compassion? Nothing good, you can be sure! Unfortunately, this is exactly what is happening in communities all across America and it has become a very serious problem.

Absent a competent trail guide and the positive reinforcement that follows, boys never make the proper passage to becoming a man. The wound is inflicted when the father fails to show up, or if he conveys to his son, "You're not good enough!" While a mother is the most important person in a boy's early life, when he reaches puberty he looks to his dad. Only his father or other qualified male surrogate can speak the words a boy longs to hear—"Yes, you *are* good enough!" Only real men have the qualifications to lead a boy through the steps of authentic initiation. Because of his position, however, no one can wound a boy in the center of his heart like his father can.

Forgiving your son

A wise father sees the reflection of himself in his son, remembering that he too is a sinner—a prodigal child of God. If you want to explore the subtle genius of the painter's artistry, try this: Google "Rembrandt's prodigal son," and spend a few moments looking into the old man's face. Besides his warm, compassionate countenance, there is something else about him that only a very imaginative artist could have captured with a paintbrush. A close up look reveals that, while his left eye appears fixed on his repentant son, his right eye is looking toward the source of the light on his face. This is a beacon of love, a light from Eternity. The old man once knelt in the same place where his son now kneels; he too, was in need of Grace. He remembers, and filled with joy, he utters the words "I forgive you." These are the words he prayed he could one day speak to his son, for you see, he had already forgiven him in his heart. Forgiveness begets forgiveness, love begets love.

As a young man, Rembrandt lived a life much like that of the prodigal son. His early self-portraits reveal a rebel, seduced by the myriad pleasures of life. But by the time he painted *The Return of the Prodigal Son*, he had repented of this lifestyle. In the painting, he depicted God in the figure of the old man and painted himself as the penitent son. This was his way of making a public confession, while recognizing that forgiveness had come from his Father in Heaven. Brilliant!

The prodigal daughter

In 2007, I had a chance meeting with someone from another planet. His name is Cort Heibert and he has dedicated his life to rescuing souls from the abyss of brokenness.[8] Heibert had been eavesdropping on a conversation I was having with a friend about the book I was writing, when he walked over to me and declared, "I have had a lot of amazing experiences in the mountains!" I soon discovered that he was not exaggerating. He proceeded to recount astonishing tales of fall and redemption, which became great material for *Lessons of the Wild*. This "man from Mars" phoned me the following week, eager to tell me more about his adventures. "I have to tell you about a hooker I once took to the mountains," he exclaimed. My curiosity was aflame when we got together a few days later. Cort began, "I was having breakfast at a local restaurant before setting out on a five-day camping

---

[8] Andersen, *Lessons of the Wild*. Read about Cort Heibert's incredible tales of adventure, beginning at page 90.

trip when I noticed a young woman seated at a nearby table, who was by all appearances a prostitute. She looked like she was down on her luck, so I asked her if she wanted something to eat. She accepted my invitation and joined me at my table. When she asked where I was headed, I explained that I was going camping for a few days in the San Bernardino Mountains. Then, I blurted out, 'Wanna go?'" They must have made a curious pair that evening as they sat by the campfire—a wilderness evangelist and a streetwalker dressed in high heels and dime store jewelry.

For several days Cort and the young woman just talked, while nature worked her magic. She had many questions about Heibert's family, his attraction to nature and his faith in a Higher Power. She offered him sex, but it wasn't sex that he wanted. When they returned to the city, the woman confessed, "I don't want to go back to the streets." Cort offered to let her stay with him in his rented motel room for a short time until she could make other living arrangements. Then one day he returned from work to find her neatly dressed and packed to leave. "I need one more favor," she said. When asked if she needed money, she responded, "No, I need a ride to the bus station. I've made peace with my family. I'm going home." He drove the woman to a Greyhound bus station and said goodbye. He never saw her again.

When he returned to the motel, Cort picked up the tattered old Bible that he had given to the ex-hooker to read. When he opened it, he found its pages teeming with her notes and reflections—the tracks of a seeker in uncharted territory. From the markings, it was obvious that certain passages dealing with friends and family relationships had been read many times over. Day after day in the solitude of the motel room the woman pondered her grave humiliation, her deep loneliness. Somewhere in that quiet space she found forgiveness. Then, the prodigal daughter chose to "make peace" with her parents and return home.

At this point of the book, we are getting very close to the essential nature of forgiveness.

> *What wolf do you feed?*

6

THE GREATEST SECRET

*"Light of the world, shine on me. Love is the answer.
Shine on us all, set us free. Love is the answer."*
ENGLAND DAN & JOHN FORD COLEY

The most recognizable phrase in the United States Constitution is probably the dictum that all people have an inalienable right to "the pursuit of happiness." *WisdomGuides*© suggests that true happiness is something, not that we achieve by pursuit, but rather *ensues* from gratefulness living. We firmly believe that the recipe for happiness starts with being fully in the present, nurturing an abiding appreciation for all that's right with our lives. This recipe for a happy life seems straightforward enough, but the meaning of the word "happiness" is not easily arrived at. Happiness seems to be one of those states of being that you must experience for yourself before you can adequately describe what it is or how it feels.

Not long ago, I was sitting in the waiting room at a medical clinic, when a man of about seventy walked in. After he checked in with the receptionist, he turned and walked toward an empty seat in the crowded room.

As he sat down, he exclaimed to the stranger next to him, "You don't look happy!" Looking surprised, the stranger replied, "Uh. . . no, I'm happy. What about you?" Fumbling with his cell phone, the first man admitted, "I'm not happy." Trying to comfort the unhappy patient, the stranger said, "Well at least you have an iPhone. That's one reason to be happy." After hearing this brief exchange, I barely resisted the urge to burst out laughing. The cheerless man went on to provide the entire waiting room with the details of his declining health, concluding with, "Growing old is a bitch!"

This is the story of a man who is having trouble accepting the fact that he is aging, so he projects his unhappiness onto other people. When he said "You don't look happy," he really meant to say "I'm not a happy person. Can you empathize with me?" Like the man in the waiting room, living in our past only perpetuates unhappiness and causes us to "live in distress." Distress is both the effect and the cause of living in the past. We find ample evidence that each and every one of us lives in the tension between stress and distress. Stress is anything that causes wear and tear on the body and our systems. Even healthy actions like thinking, eating, drinking, talking and playing create stress. We slide along the continuum from stress toward distress when our psychological needs are not being met and we fall into the trap of afflictive emotion. People living in distress are not happy.

Radio talk show host and lecturer Dennis Prager proposes in *Happiness is a Serious Problem* that happiness is not only a goal, but a moral obligation. Prager asserts that happiness can actually be measured by looking at *un*-happiness. To illustrate this idea, he developed the formula below.

$$U \text{ (Unhappiness)} = I \text{ (Self-image)} - R \text{ (Reality)}$$

Prager explains how a distorted self-image can lead to a crisis for middle aged men. Perhaps this is a clue to why our man in the waiting room is so unhappy.

> Images are a major source of men's "midlife crisis." By a certain age many men realize that what they have achieved professionally falls short of the image they had of what they would achieve by that age. The difference between the two forms much of that "crisis."[1]

This formula might be restated to say that a man's level of unhappiness can be measured by the disparity between his false self and his True Self. To expose this "happiness gap," he must take the inner path of self-discovery. If he is brutally honest and accepts himself for who he is, he has begun to bridge the divide between fantasy and reality. Self-accepting people are happier because they know how to negotiate the treacherous terrain between who they truly are and who they only pretend to be. They are realistic about their personal qualities and attributes, and they are conscious of their human shortcomings and failings. When they look around, they see their brokenness reflected in the lives of other people. Such persons develop the capacity for vulnerability and subsequently they are inclined to be forgiving. Conversely, those who are hiding from themselves are more likely to be judgmental and blaming of others. These folks have been conditioned to look outside of themselves for the sources of their unhappiness. People in this latter category are not very good at forgiveness. They become more and more like the unhappy man in the waiting room.

---

[1] Dennis Prager, *Happiness is a Serious Problem, A Human Nature Repair Manual* (New York: Harper Collins, 1998), 27.

Inner life

If someone says to you, "I have a spiritual life," you would probably interpret it to mean that they go to church or follow certain religious practices like prayer or Bible study. What about people who claim to have experience with an "inner life," or, as the Quaker would say, the "Inner Light"? Secularists explain away these "experiences" as nothing more than figments of an overactive imagination, triggered by emotional and psychological need. To the contrary, Tom and I have met (and continue to meet) more people than we can number who lead life from the inside out, from a deep spiritual center. This inner life is not separate from, but beautifully integrated as part of our whole created being—body, mind and spirit.

Over time, trends in Western culture have devalued the importance of spirituality in leading a happy and fulfilling life. People living today seem to have adopted a different mindset than our ancestors, and perhaps more than ever before we tell our story by way of externals. We often let our careers define who we are, demonstrating to the world that we are engaged in meaningful work. We exhibit our treasures to advertise that we are relevant and have the goods to prove it. We associate with a certain class of people to broadcast that we have power and influence. We allow ourselves to be consumed by the news media, which maneuvers us into adopting someone else's worldview, biases and advocacies. All of these are subconscious means to attach meaning to our lives. And so it goes. . . we live and breathe in a milieu of external significance.

One of the most vivid examples of how we outwardly tell our story can be seen in the growing fascination with tattoos. According to one source, there are now more than 21,000 tattoo parlors in the U.S., patronized by the more than forty million adults who have at least one tattoo. It was once the province of masculinity, but now more women (23 percent) than men (19 percent) are sporting tattoos. While Americans are the tattoo trend setters, Europeans are also getting "inked" at a record pace. The business has attracted a generation of fine arts school graduates who have not found traditional employment and have resorted to tattooing as a means of self-expression.[2]

What is going on to account for the widespread phenomenon of the tattoo? A report in *The Guardian*, a leading liberal news agency headquartered in Britain, carried this revealing explanation:

> A tattoo gives you something to live for. Why do you get up in the morning? To wear grey, to have your life ruled by train timetables? A tattoo offers you something personal and fun and exciting in a world that can be drab and grey. People's souls are crying out for that. Tattoos are great for finding out more about yourself, for meeting people, for getting up in the morning and looking in the mirror and thinking: look at that! A work of art, in progress.[3]

It is important to recognize that our discussion of tattoos comes, not from a place of judgement, but as encouragement for readers to think about why they have chosen to get inked or pierced.[4] When it comes to human motivation, *WisdomGuides©* operates from this unassailable behavioral tenet: *All behavior is designed to get us something we want.* This implies that we

---

[2] https://www.factretriever.com/tattoo-facts. This site reports that the tattoo industry in the U.S. has grown to more than 1.6 billion dollars in annual revenues, (December 30, 2017).
[3] Jon Henley, *The Guardian*, https://www.theguardian.com/artanddesign/2010/jul/20/tattoos, (December 7, 2017).
[4] A Web search turns up some interesting reasons for why people choose to get tattoos.

believe something is missing from our lives, or that our situation would improve if we had more of something. While we cannot presume to know the "why-behind" another person's choices, we can be certain of one thing: when we choose to grow a beard, dye our hair, or carry a protest sign, we want something. Where does this "want" emanate from?

We suggest that tattoos, like all forms of body modification, are outward manifestations of genuine feelings we have about ourselves and the people and events of our lives. It is our unique story, told in clear and compelling fashion for everyone to see. In no uncertain terms, we want the world to know about (and acknowledge) our loves and joys and pains and sorrows. A tattoo becomes part of our identity and for many people it "gives them something to live for."

Father Greg Boyle is the founder of Homeboy Industries, dedicated to helping at-risk youth avoid gangs and make better lives for themselves. If you want to understand the deeper significance of the image you see on someone's flesh, read *Tattoos on the Heart*.[5] If Father Boyle teaches us anything through this book, it is that *until we connect our outer self with our inner being, we will not live a life of integrity*. We will continue to see all of life as a "drab and grey" existence, "ruled by train timetables." Yes, our souls are "crying out!" But they are crying out, not for more outer... they are crying out for more *inner*. The tattoos on your heart will tell you more about yourself than the ones on your arm.

We wrote this section with the hope that you will consider investing as much time, strength and intensity in your "inner" as you do in your "outer." We passionately maintain that your connection with an inner life will sustain you when times get tough,

---

[5] Gregory Boyle, *Tattoos on the Heart, The Power of Boundless Compassion* (New York: Free Press, 2010).

making it easier for you to forgive someone and ask for forgiveness in return. External expression is fine as far as it goes, but we think you will be happiest when you lead your life from the inside-out, from your deep spiritual center.

Queen of Virtue

Gratefulness is the quintessential building block for happiness; it is the "Queen of Virtue." We cannot be truly happy unless we recognize the abundance of life's blessings—friends, family, food, shelter, security and all the rest. Remember, *it is possible to be grateful and not happy, but it is impossible to be happy and not grateful.* Gratitude adds up and it rubs off on the people we meet.

For years, I shopped at the small liquor store conveniently located near our suburban neighborhood. Whenever I stopped by the store, I could count on being warmly greeted by the owners, Ralph and his brother Leonard. Although their prices weren't the lowest, the store had the loyal following of almost every household in the area. Without fanfare or prior notice, the brothers abruptly sold the business and dropped out of sight. Ten years had gone by when I bumped into Ralph again at a friend's wedding reception. When he saw me, he could hardly restrain himself, saying: "It's so great to see you. I have to tell you something. You were one of the nicest people we ever met. You were so very kind to us. Thank you for being such a great customer." I was almost in tears as I listened to his sincere expression of gratitude. When I sat down at my table I couldn't resist telling my wife and friends what Ralph had said to me. I was somewhat embarrassed to learn that he had delivered the very same message to nearly every former customer in the room. Nevertheless, I still felt special that he took the time to single me out for being a nice person. Men and women like Ralph, who exude a spirit of love and generosity, infect everyone around them with positive energy.

Is there a connection between the emotions experienced in gratefulness and the feelings that form the conditions necessary for forgiveness? Surely, there is a reason why people like Ralph so easily vocalize their thanks, while many of the rest of us have a hard time showing our gratitude. (Think of how many opportunities are missed each day to verbalize gratitude and find forgiveness in our hearts!)

Many years ago, Tom conducted a workshop for a business group on the value of expressing gratitude and celebrating success in the workplace. He remembers saying, "Isn't it a shame that gratitude isn't taught." Since then things have changed and the power of gratitude is no longer a secret. In the emerging Science of Gratitude there are numerous corporate consultants who now teach the subject to their client companies. Countless self-help books have been written on the psychology of gratitude and some devotees even carry around "gratitude rocks" or other symbols to remind them to practice gratefulness more intentionally.

A major survey of 2,000 people commissioned by the Templeton Foundation in 2012 reported these telling facts about gratitude:[6]

- Women express gratitude far more often than men (52 to 44 percent).

- Eighteen to twenty-four year olds are least likely to show gratitude, and when they do it is largely self-serving, in the hopes that people will be nicer to them.

---

[6] Visit The John Templeton Foundation website, https://www.templeton.org/, (March 8, 2018). There are numerous articles and resources on the Web for applying the research to an everyday practice of gratitude.

- Friends and freedom top the list of things people are grateful for.
- In the workplace, only ten percent of people thanked their colleagues. A major reason for this is the concern that co-workers could take advantage of them if they appeared to be vulnerable or weak.
- Eighty-one percent of people surveyed said they would work harder for a grateful boss. [Antonyms for grateful are "unappreciative" and "thankless." How much fun is it to work for that kind of boss?]

Janice Kaplan reported on the Templeton project and in her bestselling *The Gratitude Diaries* she revealed that people who declare themselves to be "religious or spiritual" tend to be more grateful than those who are not. She also discovered that married couples are more grateful than single people.[7] Another major study found that "gratitude letter writing" reduced depression in patients by more than forty percent.[8]

What about the impact a gratefulness mindset has on our children? Youngsters who are taught the meaning of gratitude develop stronger, richer relationships as they grow up. They are happier, do better in school and are less envious and materialistic than their peers. A happy child is never bored and parents do well who involve their kids in service activities, teaching them to be grateful for the opportunity to be of help to someone else, with the expectation of nothing in return.

All this data leads us to conclude that the practice of gratitude is good for us and can be learned. Keeping a gratitude journal, writing letters of appreciation and performing random acts of kindness promote a better

---

[7] Janice Kaplan, *The Gratitude Diaries: How a Year Looking on the Bright Side Can Transform Your Life* (New York: Dutton, 2015).
[8] Center of Excellence for Research and Training in Integrative Health at U.C. San Diego, http://cim.ucsd.edu/research/, (March 8, 2018).

self-image. This leads to reduced depression, more achievement/goal directed success, the will to exercise more and eat healthier, a decline in abuse of alcohol and narcotics, and lower blood pressure. Not only does the practice of gratefulness benefit our physical and emotional health, but it also enhances our spiritual well-being by making it much easier to become forgiving persons. People who are filled with gratitude pour themselves into the world and infuse it with goodness.[9]

The standard meaning of gratitude is the affirmation of goodness; the recognition that there is good outside of ourselves. Feelings of gratefulness start when we realize that we have received something of value from another person and acknowledging what it cost them. Sincere gratitude is experienced in "otherness," the awareness that the "other" has freely given of themselves in ways that have made our lives better. This awareness happens through insight, by taking time to count our blessings and realize that what we have is enough. This is what gratitude is all about and why people like Ralph are so important to the world.

Speedbumps and roadblocks

Why aren't there more "Ralphs" to brighten up our lives and help make us happy? We see a number of obvious roadblocks, some of which are natural and unavoidable, and others that are of our own doing. These roadblocks create gridlock on our hearts and delay movement toward expressions of gratitude. We propose that these same obstacles restrict the freedom of spirit that gives rise to forgiveness.

---

[9] At the back of this book on page 193, you will find instructions for making a "Grateful Box." This simple little box becomes a repository for all the gratitude you feel when you take time to remember how lucky you are to be you.

The main "speedbump" on the road to gratitude and forgiveness is our ego.[10] We spend the first thirty-five years or so of our lives building a strong ego that compares and competes and is the source of all conflict. The ego conspires, condemns and crucifies with impunity, seeking to gain personal advantage wherever it can. Richard Rohr claims, "The ego prefers the economy of merit, where we divide the world into winners and losers. . . An economy of merit cannot process free love or free anything."[11]

Clearly, it is important for us to build a strong ego. It is from our egos that we acquire and nurture the competencies we give to the world, such as in the work we do. The ego is the source of our self-image and our belief in ourselves; and it is through our egos that we develop habits to protect and defend ourselves. But, if we have a "win/lose" approach to life, as many of us do in our early adult lives, how likely are we to earnestly express gratitude and learn the art of forgiveness?

When the ego gets out of control it causes overattachments to what we see "out there" in the world. We compare ourselves to others and as a result we let our identity be defined by someone else. This lands us squarely on the trail to unhappiness. The ego "majors in the minors," where we are bothered by inconsequential stuff that is completely beyond our control. As Tom is wont to say, "When our ego is in charge we are stuck on stupid." If this is not clear to you, take a moment to think about the people in your life—especially in your youth—who modeled unpleasant manifestations of an out of control ego. Clearly, such ego driven behavior by people who should have been

---

[10] A "speedbump" is any condition that adversely affects our psyche. "Roadblocks" are barriers that prevent us from getting to a better place in our lives.

[11] Richard Rohr, "An Economy of Grace," https://cac.org/an-economy-of-grace-2017-05-23/, (May 23, 2017).

better role models was not helpful to you in your personal development.

What positive role models do we presently have in our society? Do we find them in academia, in the halls of government, or in the media? Where is gratitude expressed and instilled as an important value in our young people? What speedbumps do you see in your own life?

When we become young adults, our ego is supposed to be on fire, ready to do good things and make a difference for the world. But by then many of us have been conditioned to withhold our feelings and expressions of thankfulness. Too often we have not been taught how forgiveness works. We have been weaned away from these caring, loving practices which are the essential ingredients for a happy life. The really bad news is that many of us hang onto our egos well into adulthood. We ingrain bad habits that were meant to be overcome as we grew older. So the same conditions that held us back when we were young hold us back in maturity, too.

Who we are today is of course a combination of the way we came into the world (our "nature") and our early subconscious interpretation of the environment we grew up in ("nurture"). All humans have essential, innate qualities, our "essence," that can be speedbumps to retard us from moving toward the grace of gratitude and forgiveness. Some people come into the world as optimists by nature, while others are naturally more pessimistic. While we don't have irrefutable evidence, we see a strong correlation between pessimism and the capacity to forgive. Pessimists have a bumpy road ahead.

The way we were nurtured has a great deal to do with our ability to be happy. Someone who had a difficult upbringing can still choose to be happy, but only if they remain mindful, self-aware and intentional about it. We have to live consciously. Our brains must stay engaged, or our nature will govern our behavior.

The brain is hard-wired in a certain way and has a natural tendency to see incoming stimuli from a negative perspective. You could liken the brain to a kind of "Velcro" for the negative. To illustrate, consider a simple interaction that Tom had with a stranger following baseball's 2017 World Series. The Los Angeles Dodgers, after their most successful season in thirty years, had just been defeated by the Houston Astros in a climactic seventh game. Tom was having breakfast at his favorite diner when a man with a Dodger jersey, pushing a baby stroller, walked by. Tom remarked, "Now wasn't that a terrific season?" Expressing his disappointment, the man dourly replied, "Until the last game."

Our emotions form a storehouse for our memories. This man is unhappy about the final outcome and may remember this baseball season with dissatisfaction and dismay. Unfortunately, he may miss the feeling of gratitude for the thrills and excitement that the team generated for Dodger fans in 2017. Later on, he might even pass along his negative feelings to his son. Because of our Velcro brains, we too easily add conditions to our happiness?

Most people live with background static, what we call "internal noise," which hums away in our brains and distracts us from living in the present moment. Examples are nervousness (abnormal anxiety), worry, boredom and a general dissatisfaction with the way things are. Our internal noise surreptitiously invites us into a place of general discontentment, where it is easy to focus more on what we don't have than what we do have. We think that when you listen to most television and radio programming, to our politicians and to most educators in our colleges and universities, you are being taught to focus on what is lacking. We rarely find the hopeful encouragement that is so necessary to be thankful and forgiving?

Another source of internal noise is the image we have of ourselves. Do you have a realistic sense of who you are, or do you tend to be too hard on yourself? Do you get overly concerned when you can't do things perfectly? Does your head get polluted with "I should have" messages? How often do you make comparisons between yourself and other people? It is said, "We become what we think." When you think about what you are lacking and what you wish you had, you hit a big roadblock.

When we ask a room full of people, "Is conflict good or bad," what do you suppose is the overwhelming response? After decades of asking this question, we have found than more than ninety percent of respondents will emphatically respond, "Bad!" This widespread misunderstanding puts us way behind in winning at the game of life. When conflict arises, this outlook invariably leads to attack and defend; in other words, a lose/lose approach. Conflict is healthy because it invites us to be a participant, rather than a bystander in getting us or our team or our world to a better place.

All human interaction is either relationship building or relationship damaging. Human connection is one of the most important of our primal human needs, so when conflicts get resolved, it makes for better relationships among the people involved. When conflict arises, we encourage you to walk toward it. Choose not to die "with your back to the enemy." And if you consider yourself an agent for real change in the world, then work at eliminating one of the main sources of societal disharmony—*intergenerational conflict. Do your best to understand and accept the values of generations outside of your own.* You will be glad you did!

Distress is fed by chronic anxiety and worry. Like oil and water, it cannot co-exist in harmony with a gratefulness/forgiveness mentality. Here are some of the ways distress manifests itself:

- Acting from a place of shame, guilt, or apathy
- The need to complete things too perfectly
- The frustration of being an "over-pleaser"
- Living by the word "should," or judgement without action
- Unresolved grief
- Anger that cannot be let go of, or expressed in a healthy way
- Fear that engulfs us, resulting in inaction
- Living in the past

Our work confirms our suspicion that most of us are in distress most of the time. Even if this is an exaggeration, at least you must admit there is a lot of distress going around. Distress seems to us to be more than your standard roadblock to happiness.

At this point of the book you should have a good grasp of what we mean by unfinished business, which we crown "the mother of all gridlock." In one of life's great ironies, we will not see unfinished business in someone else unless it is also present in us. We see brokenness most clearly through our own broken lens. When a trait in another person bothers us, it is because we have our own unfinished business to deal with. Our natural inclination is then to project our garbage onto the other person in the form of judgement, blame and the general absence of taking responsibility.

We sometimes ask participants in our workshops questions like, "Do people out there in the world take things personally? Have you ever taken anything personally?" No one ever answers, "No!" Why? Why bother to take offense? What does it serve? We suggest to you that nothing is really personal; it is only made so by our interpretations. These interpretations are speedbumps, directly linked to our past through memories stored in our emotional repositories. Instead of responding by taking something personally, what else could we do? The simple answer is to consciously dis-identify with the "incoming" and see it as just information. This takes our emotions out of the picture and makes it easier for us to decide if we want to do something about what happened. The practice of dis-identification is something that takes some effort to learn, but is a major stress reducer.[12]

If we put up roadblocks and lay down speedbumps, we are effectively placing ourselves under attack. We will not be using our conscious mind, but only reacting to what we see in front of us. Hence, we will not differentiate ourselves from the rest of the world in any helpful way. We will be just like all the other frogs swimming along in the warm comfort of the stove pot.

Hopefully, you are no longer asking yourself why there are so few "Ralphs" to teach us kindness and gratefulness. Each of us must seek and discover ways to get past the gridlock on our hearts and nurture conditions necessary for us to feel and express gratitude and forgiveness. This is the movement from ego to *Grace*, made perfect by the greatest power in the universe. This radical transformation happens because of. . .

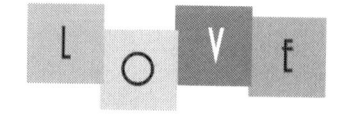

L O V E

---

[12] Some of the concepts in this section have been borrowed and adapted from leading thinkers in the field of psychology and human motivation. For example, the list at the top of page 119 was derived in part from the work of Taibi Kahler, Ph.D.

The secret of forgiveness

For much of the world, Jesus Christ is the embodiment of love perfected. For no apparent material reward or financial gain, he spent his life in service to others. So big was his love that he submitted himself to torture and death, all in the name of friendship. He told those closest to him, "No one has greater love than this: to lay down one's life for one's friends."[13] Jesus' message of peace and reconciliation still reverberates around the world, with Christians and non-Christians alike. From one of his dedicated early followers we have the following words, which have been spoken at countless weddings throughout the ages:

> Love is patient, love is kind. It does not envy, it does not boast, it is not proud. It does not dishonor others, it is not self-seeking, it is not easily angered, it keeps no record of wrongs. Love does not delight in evil but rejoices with the truth. It always protects, always trusts, always hopes, always perseveres.[14]

This hymn of Christian love comes down to us from a first century Pharisee[15], whose given name was Saul. The hatemongering Saul was one of the chief persecutors of Jesus' disciples, who in those days were called "Followers of the Way." After tracking down many of these Followers and bringing them bound to Jerusalem, Saul received authority from the high priest to go to Damascus in Syria and round up any Christians he could find there. As he neared the city, he was struck by a "light from heaven," which instantly

---

[13] John, 15:13.
[14] 1 Corinthians, 13:4–8. Written by St. Paul to the Christian community at Corinth.
[15] Pharisees were a powerful elitist religious sect that gained a reputation for piety and self-righteousness.

blinded him. But after three days, one of the men of the Way miraculously healed him and Saul's eyesight returned. But because of his peculiar ordeal, his heart was completely transformed and Saul, now known as Paul, became the principal expositor of Jesus' teachings.[16] He established numerous churches throughout the Mediterranean world, one of which was in the ancient city of Corinth. In his absence, the church there developed a serious crisis of leadership, so Paul wrote letters to the Corinthians in hopes of resolving their differences. His letters have all the elements necessary for a lasting reconciliation: patience, kindness, trustworthiness, hopefulness and perseverance. Paul pointed out that love is not prideful, disrespectful, selfish, or angry. Such love is the antidote for the afflictive emotions. Love cures all!

Paul's efforts at reconciliation with the Corinthian community did not meet with immediate success. However, with the help of its dedicated leaders, the church rebounded and became one of the great incubators of the Christian faith. This was not achieved by typical political wrangling and power brokering. Jesus had given his disciples a simple litmus test for fidelity when he said to them, "A new command I give you: Love one another. As I have loved you, so you must love one another. By this everyone will know that you are my disciples, if you love one another."[17] Paul had only to affirm the power of love to reconcile with his brothers and sisters at Corinth.

Take one last look at *The Return of the Prodigal Son*. The background is dark and shadowy, nearly consuming the two servants depicted in the painting. The light shining on the faces of the father and his recalcitrant son is intensified by the blackness surrounding it. The light, of course, is the light of pure Love—the beacon

---

[16] Acts, 9:1–22.
[17] John, 13:34–5.

that breaks through the darkness of sin and fills the holes in men's souls. Such a powerful light-force can emanate only from Heaven. The son cannot escape this celestial beam, and like the thieves hanging on wooden crosses next to Jesus, he must make his choice. In the Biblical parable, the reader is left to wonder if he ever forgave his father for favoring his prodigal brother. But there is one thing we know for certain. The father openly expressed his unconditional love for both sons when he told the elder, "We had to celebrate and rejoice, because this brother of yours was dead and has come to life; he was lost and has been found."[18]

Herein resides the great conundrum of forgiveness. Only when we do something wrong are we in need of forgiveness. While loyalty may receive no great tribute, there is a gala celebration for the sinner who repents. Perhaps it is our human failing that we tend to withhold the full expression of our love until something bad happens.

The impossible possibility

Theologian Reinhold Niebuhr amplifies for us how radical love is the engine of forgiveness and reconciliation:

> The crown of Christian ethics is the doctrine of forgiveness. In it the whole genius of prophetic religion is expressed. Love as forgiveness is the most difficult and impossible of moral achievements. Yet it is a possibility if the impossibility of love is recognized and the sin in the self is acknowledged. Therefore an ethic culminating in an impossible possibility produces its choicest fruit in terms of the doctrine

---

[18] Luke, 15:32.

of forgiveness, the demand that the evil in the other shall be borne without vindictiveness because the evil in the self is known.[19]

Niebuhr mined the human heart and struck gold when he unearthed this deep secret of forgiveness. *Without true love, true forgiveness never happens.* Niebuhr's paradoxical observation about the "impossible possibility" is particularly disturbing to those who are unfamiliar with Jesus' teachings. Jesus taught that we must take the introspective journey into our deep interior, where we find that we are not the person we project to the world. Jesus well knew that if a man gains insight into his own brokenness, he will be able to bear the burden of another man's wrongdoings. This is precisely what Carl Jung alluded to when he made the unsettling assertion, "I discover that I am the most impudent of all the offenders. I myself am the enemy who must be loved." Niebuhr takes this discovery a step further when by reminding us that forgiveness is not only possible, it is necessary if one is to call themselves a Christian.

Perhaps the foremost example of the possibility of the impossible is found in the life of the peacemaker. Known as the father of his nation, Mahatma Gandhi (1869–1948) employed a strategy of non-violent civil disobedience to help India gain its independence. As a young man, Gandhi left India for London, where he studied law with the intention of becoming a barrister. Upon returning home, he experienced a series of personal misfortunes, so he set sail for South Africa. There, he became a political activist for the rights of Indians living under the oppressive British regime. Gandhi eventually went back to India, where he preached and practiced nonviolence, inspiring a civil

---

[19] Reinhold Niebuhr, *An Interpretation of Christian Ethics* (Louisville, KY: Westminster John Knox Press, 2013), 223.

rights movement around the world. Because of his skin color and outspoken activism, Gandhi was systematically bullied and abused by white imperialists. In 1942, when he demanded that Britain "Quit India," he was placed under house arrest, where he remained for two years. Gandhi ultimately prevailed in his quest for liberty, and under his leadership India became a free nation in 1947. But the bitter, protracted struggle had deeply scarred the country and left the great peacemaker in declining health.

When asked why he wasn't a Christian, Gandhi is reputed to have said: "I like your Christ; I do not like your Christians. Your Christians are so unlike your Christ."[20] While many people took offense at this, Gandhi correctly pointed out the hypocrisy of claiming to be a Christian, but not acting as one. We could easily argue that Gandhi came closer to achieving the impossible possibility than his Christian counterparts. He tirelessly advocated for women's rights and religious freedom for people of every faith tradition. When violence erupted, he quelled it with a pure heart and a steady hand. Gandhi may not have been a Christian, but he religiously followed Jesus' commandment to love his enemies. What do you suppose he did when it came time to forgive those who had persecuted him and oppressed his people for so long?

Mahatma Gandhi has become an almost surreal figure, living in the mist of some long ago dream world. What about today? Do any of our contemporaries achieve the impossible? Perhaps!

Some years ago, I called a former colleague from my time in the corporate world. After we traded a few reminiscences of "the good old days," I asked "Gary" what he was doing to stay busy, figuring he would tell

---

[20] Frank Raj, *The Washington Times*, "Gandhi glimpsed Christ, rejecting Christianity as a false religion," http://www.washingtontimes.com/news/2014/dec/31/gandhi-glimpsed-christ-rejecting-christianity-fals/?page=all, (December 31, 2014).

me how his golf game had improved or how many grandkids he had. I was intrigued when he said, "My wife and I have a ministry and we have made several trips to the Middle East. Last time we smuggled two hundred and twenty Bibles into Iraq." I replied, "Isn't that kind of dangerous?" "Yeah, sure it is," he said. "But we are already making plans for our next trip over there." Then Gary told me a story that was difficult to believe.

He arrived in the Middle East as part of his church's outreach to persecuted believers in the region. He was greeted by his host, a priest who had arranged several discreet gatherings to share the Gospel message with the local community. During his visit, Gary's guide told him of a powerful leader he knew, who had recently converted from Islam to Christianity. Gary had heard that some Iraqi Muslims were becoming Christians, but this account was out of the ordinary. It seems the convert had once been one of the world's most wanted terrorist leaders. Gary asked his host if he could arrange a meeting with "Mr. X," and within a day or two a black limousine pulled up to where they were staying. Gary and his host got into the vehicle and without blindfolds or other security precautions were driven to a magnificent palace which stood all by itself in the middle of the desert. The palace was unlike anything Gary had ever seen before. It had polished marble pillars and exquisitely tiled floors, but there was almost no furniture to be seen. What was quite visible, however, were a number of heavily armed guards, equipped with AK-47's and other sophisticated weaponry.

The two men were promptly ushered into a meeting room, where Mr. X was waiting to greet them. He was happy to see Gary's host, and they shared a few pleasantries before Mr. X turned to his American guest. As they were formally introduced to one another, Gary asked Mr. X if he could ask him a couple of questions. He obligingly replied, "Ask anything you want." First, Gary inquired why so much security was needed at the palace. Mr. X explained that he was living in no man's land and the heavy armaments were necessary for protection against both western operatives and Muslim extremists. Most of all, Gary wanted to know how and why he came to adopt Christianity. During their conversation, Gary's host asked Mr. X about his brother, who was serving time in prison. Mr. X disclosed that, while his brother was widely thought to be the leader of the terrorist group, he had been but second in command. Mr. X was its former kingpin. This revelation floored Gary's host, who immediately asked for a sidebar conversation. The two men moved to another part of the room, where Gary observed their emotional exchange. The former adversaries embraced before returning to their seats. On the return trip, Gary asked his host if he could tell him what was said in the private conversation with Mr. X. His host revealed, "He told me, 'Only through the love of Jesus Christ could bitter enemies like us become friends.'" Had this story come from just about anyone else, I wouldn't have believed it.

You are probably familiar with the popular television series *The Twilight Zone*, which aired on CBS from 1959 to 1965. Host Rod Serling introduced the weekly show this way, "There is a fifth dimension beyond that which is known to man. It is a dimension as vast as space and as timeless as infinity. It is the middle ground between light and shadow, between science and superstition, and it lies between the pit of man's fears and the summit of his knowledge. This is the dimension of imagination. It is an area which we call the Twilight Zone." People like Mr. X live in a twilight zone, where the impossible becomes a timeless possibility.

Why is the ideal of pure love so seldom achieved? Perhaps it is because our emotional programs for happiness attach too many conditions to the free workings of love. Nevertheless, love continues to be mankind's best last hope. Without love, there will never be harmony between enemies. A thousand years from now, we will still be fighting over the same old things, for the same inane reasons, using the same ineffectual tactics. Without the expression of radical love, reconciliation remains a meaningless word buried deep in the dictionary. True forgiveness never happens without true love.

> *What are you grateful for at this very moment?*

7

YOUR BROTHER'S KEEPER

"Darkness cannot drive out darkness: only light can do that. Hate cannot drive out hate: only love can do that."
MARTIN LUTHER KING, JR.

The Biblical record contains the following account of two brothers, who were as different as day and night. In Genesis we read that Cain, firstborn son of Adam and Eve, was jealous of his younger brother Abel and became very angry. God warned him that his anger was dangerous and needed to be brought under control, but Cain didn't listen. Overcome by his afflictive emotions, Cain led Abel into the fields and killed him. This tale had the makings of the world's first murder mystery, were it not for God's vigilant intervention. Seeing the bloodshed, God confronted Cain with the million dollar question, "Where is your brother?" Cain replied, "I don't know; am I my brother's keeper?"[1]

In one of the saddest ironies of history, we have lost the meaning of our brother. Those with whom we share a common heritage often become our bitterest enemies.

---

[1] *Genesis*, 4:9.

Following Cain's pernicious example, members of the human family are still pitted against each other in more ways than we can number; North against South, Jews against Muslims, whites against blacks, rich against poor, Democrats against Republicans, and on and on.

Perhaps few of us regard men of other races as our brothers, fewer still would say they are their brother's keeper. Being a "keeper" does not imply that we play the role of the strict boarding school headmaster. No, the keeper is one who loves his brother as himself, who cares for his brother's well-being and who holds him to account. He regards his brother as his equal, never as an inferior or subservient person. He forgives him and asks for forgiveness in return. The keeper is the good brother, who lives in right relationship with his kinfolk and with his Creator. In this chapter, we will look at five historic keepers, each of whom stepped bravely into the arena to help reunite brothers living in very different worlds. Where there has been a long history of bitter conflict, there will always be more than enough blame to go around. And where there is deep division, there will be many who need the Grace of forgiveness. Therefore, having clearly emerged as the most divisive issue in present day America, we have chosen race relations as the best place to focus our study of brotherhood lost. What follows is a view from a different angle. This is our response to the pain of racism and separation, shown so vividly in the traumatic scenes we have witnessed in places like Ferguson, Missouri.

John Woolman (1720–72)

Probably no one in a thousand has heard of John Woolman, an itinerant tailor, who was one of America's earliest abolitionists. He traveled throughout the

Colonial frontier, calling for an end to the slave trade and for the immediate release of all men forcibly held in servitude. He denounced anyone engaged in human commerce, refusing the hospitality of fellow Quakers who were slaveholders. This calling exacted a heavy toll on Woolman, whose diary exposed a man struggling mightily to be a faithful servant of a greater Master. Here is a brief passage from *The Journal of John Woolman*, dated May 13, 1757:

> As I was riding along in the morning my mind was deeply affected in a sense I had of the need of Divine aid to support me in the various difficulties which attended me, and in the uncommon distress of mind I cried in secret to the Most High, "Oh Lord, be merciful, I beseech thee, to Thy poor afflicted creature!"[2]

While he suffered humiliation and ridicule at the hands of his own people, Woolman clearly saw a vision of himself reflected in the faces of his oppressed brothers. When he censured slaveholding Friends, he was told that human bondage was Biblically justifiable, that the Negro was a direct descendant of Cain and his dark skin was God's mark of wickedness. As payment for his sins, the black man was consigned to be a slave for all times. This spurious argument led to Scriptural sparring, where Woolman often gained the measure of his opponents. The tide of oppression finally turned toward freedom and because of John Woolman and others like him, the Quakers became the first religious organization to forbid slavery. Yet, for his remarkable achievements, Woolman always judged himself a helpless sinner in need of God's mercy.

---

[2] Thomas S. Kepler, ed., *The Journal of John Woolman* (The World Publishing Co.: 1954), 57.

William Wilberforce (1759–1833)

John Woolman wasn't the only abolitionist to make headlines for his controversial activism. On the other side of the Atlantic, a wealthy member of the English Parliament dedicated his life to ending the slave trade on the high seas. While on an extended European holiday, William Wilberforce had a spiritual awakening that marked a dramatic turn in his life. After that, he did missionary work in India, helped establish the Church Mission Society and was one of the founding fathers of The Society for the Prevention of Cruelty to Animals. Wilberforce became increasingly alarmed that British agents were raiding the African continent and selling as many as 50,000 people annually into slavery. Despite a withering attack by pro-slavery forces for almost twenty years, Wilberforce was able to get legislation passed in 1807 that forbade slave trading in the British Empire. Chronically ill, he died just three days before the passage of the Slavery Abolition Act of 1833, which ended the institution of slavery altogether. In one of his impassioned speeches before Parliament, here is what this brave man said:

> Let us not despair; it is a blessed cause, and success, ere long, will crown our exertions. Already we have gained one victory; we have obtained, for these poor creatures, the recognition of their human nature, which, for a while was most shamefully denied. This is the first fruits of our efforts; let us persevere and our triumph will be complete. Never, never will we desist till we have wiped away this scandal from the Christian name, which our posterity, looking back to the history of these enlightened times, will scarce believe that it has been

suffered to exist so long a disgrace and dishonour to this country.[3]

William Wilberforce has been immortalized in literature and in the award winning 2006 film *Amazing Grace*. "Amazing Grace," one of the world's great folk hymns, was composed more than two centuries ago by John Newton (1725–1807). Newton was a former slave trader who had a spiritual epiphany and fought alongside Wilberforce to help free his black brothers from their great travail.

Nelson Mandela (1918–2013)

By any historical account, Nelson Mandela was one of the giants of the Twentieth Century. He was born of royal roots in Africa in 1918, at the end of "The Great War." From an early age, Mandela was on a collision course with destiny. He became a leading activist to abolish racial discrimination by the colonialist South African government. Mandela joined the anti-apartheid Defiance Campaign, where he represented the interests of his fellow Africans against segregation. He was repeatedly arrested for seditious activities, culminating in his 1962 conviction for treason against the government. He served twenty-seven years in prison, until an international outcry finally led to his release in 1990. When he regained his freedom, he became a *tour de force* in eliminating apartheid and establishing multiracial elections. In 1994, Nelson Mandela was elected South Africa's first black president. When asked how he felt toward his oppressors, here is what he had to say:

---

[3] *Wikipedia*, https://en.wikipedia.org/wiki/William_Wilberforce, (March 11, 2016).

> As I walked out the door toward the gate that would lead to my freedom, I knew if I didn't leave my bitterness and hatred behind, I'd still be in prison. Forgiveness liberates the soul; it removes fear. That's why it's such a powerful weapon.[4]

After his election, Mandela made national unity his main initiative. He doggedly pursued a strategy of racial reconciliation, referring to post-apartheid South Africa as the "Rainbow Nation." He worked tirelessly for peace around the globe, and was awarded the Nobel Peace Prize in 1993. Although he had been unrighteously kept in prison for the best years of his life, he offered an olive branch to his white brothers in return. In his position, how many of us would have done the same?

Martin Luther King (1929–68)

Nelson Mandela's American contemporary in the battle for human rights was Baptist preacher Dr. Martin Luther King, Jr. He had a big dream about a land where all people would join hands and sing together the words from the old Negro spiritual, "Free at last. Free at last." Dr. King was also a recipient of the Nobel Prize, and he too operated from the place of compassion and forgiveness. What he knew that the unforgiver does not is that love and truth are the only things that can set a man permanently and unconditionally free. In one of his famous sermons, here is how he alluded to love:

---

[4] Trudy Bourgeois, *Huffington Post*, "The Greatest Gift," http://www.huffingtonpost.com/trudy-bourgeois/the-greatest-gift_b_4469297.html, (December 19, 2013).

When I speak of love I am not speaking of some sentimental and weak response. I am not speaking of that force which is just emotional bosh. I am speaking of that force which all of the great religions have seen as the supreme unifying principle of life. Love is somehow the key that unlocks the door which leads to ultimate reality.[5]

After receiving numerous death threats, Dr. King was assassinated on the balcony of a Memphis hotel on April 4, 1968. He was a one-of-a-kind historical figure. Even those sympathetic to his cause, will never truly understand the burden he must have felt in representing an entire race of people. He firmly held that Jesus provided the model for reconciliation and Gandhi the method. He reminded us that only light can drive out darkness and only love can conquer hate. Dr. King appealed to the Ultimate Reality, who is the beginning and the end of love.

Martin Luther King preached and taught from a place of deep insight into the twofold nature of humanity. As much as anyone, he understood the fact of mankind's inherited brokenness; he well knew what lurks in the holes in men's souls. In the manner of John Woolman, Martin Luther King acknowledged that he too was a sinner, in need of God's mercy. He spoke of forgiveness this way:

We must develop and maintain the capacity to forgive. *He who is devoid of the power to forgive is devoid of the power to love.* There is some good in the worst of us and some evil in the best of us. When we discover this, we are less prone to hate our enemies.[6]

---

[5] King, Jr., *Strength to Love*, x.
[6] From Dr. King's writings. Emphasis mine.

These words, spoken by one of the most courageous and influential men of our time, embody the pure essence of forgiveness and give us hope as we write this section of the book.

James Baldwin (1924–87)

James Baldwin was a prominent civil rights activist, who became the leading black writer on race in America during the 1960's and seventies. Baldwin's blunt commentary and harsh indictment of white privilege didn't make him many friends across the racial divide. He could easily be dismissed as an extremist, unless one takes the time to make a careful analysis of his writings. My reading of Baldwin reveals a man suffering through a great disillusionment. Influenced by Church teachings, he was horrified at how white Americans perpetually saw blacks as a subordinate race. In *The Fire Next Time*, Baldwin writes:

> A vast amount of the energy that goes into what we call the Negro problem is produced by the white man's profound desire not to be judged by those who are not white, not to be seen as he is, and at the same time a vast amount of the white anguish is rooted in the white man's equally profound need to be seen as he is, to be released from the tyranny of his mirror. All of us know, whether or not we are able to admit it, that mirrors can only lie, that death by drowning is all that awaits one there. It is for this reason that love is so desperately sought and so cunningly avoided. Love takes off the masks that we fear we cannot live without and know we cannot live within. I use the word

"love" here not merely in the personal sense, but as a state of being, or a state of grace.[7]

James Baldwin captured the human condition in a way that few were ready to concede—then, or now. He observed that the white man's fear of blacks is but a manifestation of his deeply rooted fears about himself. Looking in his mirror, he sees an image of himself that he wants to believe is true, but his reflection is based on a lie; it is only a chimera of a deeper, truer self. Baldwin concludes that when he looks at his black counterpart, the white man is faced with his own existential pain and brokenness. Fearing the truth of his commonality with an inferior being, he simply looks away. His black brother thus becomes the "invisible man."

Baldwin befriended leaders of the Nation of Islam, who advocated dividing the United States into two separate countries, one black and one white. He rejected this racist, segregationist approach, choosing instead to educate and influence Americans through non-violent activism and the power of his pen. Though he lived a life of disenchantment with the way things were, Baldwin saw a glimmer of light on the far horizon. "The black and the white deeply need each other here if we are really to become a nation," he said.[8]

Real reconciliation

It seems abundantly clear that black and white Americans have never properly reconciled with one another for the sins of our past. Sure, individuals of

---

[7] James Baldwin, *The Fire Next Time* (New York: The Dial Press, 1963), 109.
[8] Ibid., 111.

different races and ethnic backgrounds have made peace with one another (micro forgiveness), but we have yet to achieve a mutual accord at the broader macro level. Thus, we find ourselves in the same old place. Police killings of black citizens have exacerbated tensions in our country, and whether or not these actions have proven to be justifiable, trust between the races has receded to a low ebb.

WisdomGuides© believes that if we are ever to make any real progress in race relations in America, we must change the conversation. To illustrate what we mean, take a look at the simple model below (Figure 3). All the rhetoric and activism, even when motivated by the best of intentions, seem fixed on events that have already happened. Those in power are content to live with the *status quo*, and as long as no one creates too much of a ruckus, little is likely to change. People with

Race Relations Model ©
Copyright: WisdomGuides 2016

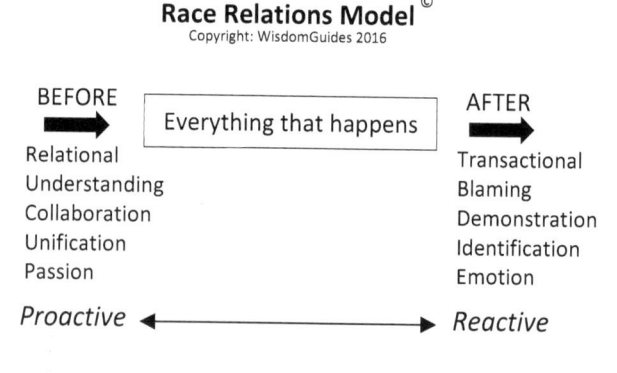

BEFORE	Everything that happens	AFTER
Relational		Transactional
Understanding		Blaming
Collaboration		Demonstration
Unification		Identification
Passion		Emotion

Proactive ←————————→ *Reactive*

Figure 3

differing perspectives banter back and forth about one situation or another. Good people take a moral stance on race relations and express their abhorrence of any kind of bigotry. Then, a significant event happens (a police shooting) that is labeled a "hate crime." Now, everyone swings into action. People identifying with the victim *again* voice outrage and organize *another* march on city hall to protest discrimination. Anti-riot units will *again* be deployed to protect the citizenry from potential violence and looting. The department may place the officer on administrative leave, pending *another* internal investigation. In most cases, the accused is exonerated by investigators, but sometimes he is fired and indicted for a criminal offense. Rarely is he convicted and sentenced to serve time in prison.

In this model, no one is ever fully satisfied with the outcome. Even when a policeman (Persecutor) is found guilty, it only confirms what people in the community (Victims) see as another example of institutional racism and homophobia. The authorities (more Persecutors) complain that they are being hindered in trying to do their job of protecting honest citizens from the bad guys. The clergy and other sympathetic leaders (Rescuers) intervene, exhausting energy and resources in trying to keep an honest dialogue going among the disparate stakeholders. In these cases, almost no one moves toward the middle. On the contrary, everyone seems to find stronger justification for their point of view. The community becomes firmly locked in their corner of the Drama Triangle.

We at *WisdomGuides*© recognize that the strained state of race relations in America can be attributed in large part to the fact that most everything is being done after the fact and not enough is happening before the "stuff hits the fan." Our country is stuck in the muck of attack and defend and we seem to be running in circles without a clear path to a permanent reconcilement.

Unity in the community

During the 2016 presidential campaign, Democratic candidate Hillary Clinton addressed a group of supporters of the controversial Black Lives Matter movement. After her speech, she was approached by a young man, who was one of the organizers. Here is a portion of the telling dialogue that transpired:

> *Activist* (clasping his hands, almost prayerfully): "I stand here in your space and I say this as respectfully as I can, but if you don't tell black people what we need to do, then we won't tell you all what to do. This is and always has been a white problem of violence. There's not much that we can do to stop the violence against us."
>
> *Mrs. Clinton*: "Well, if that is your position, then I will talk only to white people about how we are going to deal with real problems."
>
> *Activist*: "That's not what I mean. But, what you just said [in your address] was a form of victim blaming. You said what the Black Lives Matter movement needs to do to change white hearts is . . policy."
>
> *Mrs. Clinton*: "Look. I don't believe you change hearts. You change laws. You change allocation of resources. You change the way systems operate. [Then, backing off a little] You're not going to change every heart, you're not. But, at the end of the day we can do a whole lot to change some hearts, some systems . . ."[9]

The candidate went on to suggest in a rather condescending tone that the Black Lives Matter people pursue their activist agenda, while she leverages the legislative process. With this approach, she placed her political capital squarely in the AFTER side of the *WisdomGuides*© model. Note how little cooperation is

---

[9] *Majority Report* podcast, https://www.youtube.com/watch?v=hIp1Uni ZCN4, (August 19, 2015).

built into her strategy to end discrimination. Her advice is: "You keep doing what you're doing, and I will keep doing what I'm doing." This means, of course, that "we'll keep getting what we're getting." Really, is that what we want?

For his part, the activist espouses a cynical view of racial accountability and collaboration, but to his credit, he seems passionate about "changing hearts" (i.e., working in the BEFORE side of our model). AFTER side proponents seek to change behavior through legislation and compliance, while the BEFORE side depends on the power of love to bring about unity in the community. While legislation is important in structuring better communities, we at *WisdomGuides©* are staking our fortunes on something that goes much deeper in trying to solve the race problem. We believe that real healing starts when people see themselves reflected in the faces of those who don't look like them (think Mahatma Gandhi, Nelson Mandela and William Wilberforce). We know that people *can* change and we fervently maintain that cross cultural teamwork, not independent action, will get us to the promised land of racial harmony. We emphatically disagree with the B.L.M. activist that there is little that black people can do to stop the violence against them. This is the classic posture a victim (real victim, or not) takes to deny responsibility and demand payment from his persecutor. If the collaborative process is ever to gain traction in our society, individual and collective accountability will have to be acknowledged. We know that some readers will interpret this as "victim blaming." That is clearly not our intent. This book is our determined effort to illuminate the truth and "tell it like it is." We would be judged guilty if, after fairly examining our own biases, motives and actions, we do not also confront our brother with the role he plays in this terrible tragedy.

I asked a friend, a notable black activist for whom I have great respect and admiration, if he thought that Trevon Martin could have done anything in his altercation with George Zimmerman that could have resulted in his being alive today.[10] His immediate and unequivocal response was, "No." When I suggested that opposing factions should come to the table with as little emotion as they can, he bristled and said that would be impossible. I explained that passion (living in the present, informed by the past), rather than raw emotion (informed by the past, living in the past), would serve us best as we seek a brighter future together. When one or both parties in a dispute are operating from an emotional base, there cannot be a productive dialogue.

Again, anything that does not bring us together, serves to divide us. We implore our detractors and supporters alike to take a hard look in their own mirrors and then ask themselves what they are doing to build bridges, not walls. A fair question to ask yourself: "Is what I am doing merely *defining and deepening* the separation, or am I earnestly looking for ways to cross the chasm that separates me from my brother?" To paraphrase the words of Martin Luther King, "If we don't have the capacity to forgive, we won't love ourselves, or anyone else." For a very long time now, men have been on the wrong trail to rediscovering the true meaning of brotherhood. We talk about changing people's minds, but the locus of racism and bigotry is not the mind; it is the human heart. Henri Nouwen reminds us, "You don't think your way into a new kind of living. You live your way into a new kind of thinking."[11] When a man leads from his heart with

---

[10] Martin, a 17-year old black youth, was shot and killed by white security guard George Zimmerman in Sanford, Florida in 2012. Facts can be obtained from *CNN News*, http://www.cnn.com/2013/06/05/us/trayvon-martin-shooting-fast-facts/index.html, (December 16, 2017).

[11] *Goodreads*, https://www.goodreads.com/author/quotes/4837.Henri_J

wisdom and understanding, he can become all that he can be. Perhaps then his brother will also become the man God wants *him* to be.

If you want to find out why you think and feel the way you do, we recommend that you read Jonathan Haidt's *The Righteous Mind*.[12] The book presents compelling evidence that the heart rules the head, not vice versa. According to Haidt and his colleagues, judgements we make about what we see in the world are based on intuitions (feelings) that derive from our moral foundations—loyalty, sanctity, fairness, and others. We then form arguments that support our judgements, all the while convinced that we have come to our conclusions on a purely rational basis. Haidt goes on to describe "hivishness," which is the desire to be connected to a tribe, in the same way that a bee belongs to a hive. People will go to great lengths to support and defend their group, even when they are shown to be on the wrong side of the truth. Tribal fidelity becomes deeply ingrained and is the basis for the attack and defend dramas that appear in *The Truth About Forgiveness*.

You might consider testing yourself against Haidt's hypotheses. Tune to one of the cable news networks or radio talk shows that you absolutely deplore because of their "biased" reporting and "fake news" broadcasts. Are you angered and offended by the "lies, false accusations and innuendoes" you hear? Be honest! Do you see yourself getting agitated by someone you label a "shill," a "political hack," or "downright anti-American"? How likely would you be to even attempt to have an open and honest discussion with someone who espouses such "extremist" positions on the issues?

_M_Nouwen, (December 9, 2017).
[12] Jonathan Haidt, *The Righteous Mind, Why Good People Are Divided by Politics and Religion* (New York: Vintage Books, 2012). Haidt's team researched cultures around the world and determined that all of them rely on the same moral foundations from which to make judgements.

Making restitution

Senior editor for the *Atlantic* magazine Ta-Nehisi Coates makes a persuasive argument that racial reconciliation starts with African-Americans being adequately compensated for the suffering caused by the institution of slavery. Coates is a bright progressive, who has written the best-selling *Between Me and the World*. The book is tough sledding for many readers, especially when the writer addresses white supremacy and the sin of racism. Coates asserts that our leaders can be "pioneers" by making financial reparations to African-Americans; and he calls for "color blindness" to be built into our country's policy making processes.[13] Worthy though they may be, policy and legislative processes are *transactional* measures, done at a macro level. Actions of the heart operate on the micro level, on a one-to-one *relational* basis. Forgiveness and bona fide reconciliation simply cannot take place at the transactional level. A cash settlement will sustain people on a relatively short term material-empowerment basis, but will not be the impetus for lasting harmony between black and white Americans. Economic power will undoubtedly change a man's life, but no amount of money will soften his heart.[14]

In 1988, President Ronald Reagan signed the Civil Liberties Act, which compensated more than 100,000 Japanese-Americans who had been incarcerated by the U.S. military during World War II. A formal apology

---

[13] "Facing the Truth: The Case for Reparations," Moyers & Co., https://www.youtube.com/watch?v=Pm9DJuTrO8Q, (May 23, 2014).

[14] *WisdomGuides*© supports sweeping reforms to "level the playing field" and provide sustained economic opportunity for disadvantaged Americans. This calls for shared leadership by disparate stakeholders and must include unprecedented investment in education, healthcare and housing. It would be helpful if the President of the United States would make a formal acknowledgement of the moral wrongs done by the institution of slavery and begin a process that would lead to a full and final restitution.

and a twenty-thousand dollar check was issued to every known survivor of the internment camps. The Civil Liberties Act may have assuaged the guilt of some in leadership, but the cash settlement likely had little consequence for a genuine reconciliation. How much money do you think it would take to compensate someone for the humiliation and degradation they suffered in one of those camps? We suggest that no material compensation would be sufficient, begging the point made earlier (refer to page 38) that a man will never get enough of what he does not really want.

Jon was a grocery store owner in East Los Angeles at the outbreak of World War II. Being of Japanese descent, he was rounded up with members of his family and sent to one of the California internment camps, where he lived until the end of the war. I heard Jon's story from his grandson Bob, who wrote his Master's degree thesis on his grandfather's experiences during and after his incarceration. Someone he knew had kept his grocery store going until he returned home and eventually Jon opened several more stores, becoming one of the most successful grocers in Los Angeles.

Around 1970, as he did research for his thesis, Bob asked his grandfather if he resented what the U.S. government had done to him. He learned that Jon had not waited around for an apology and a big check. While not condoning the government's overreaction in imprisoning its own citizens, he let go of any ill feelings he had toward the people in power. Jon explained to Bob that through it all he never thought of himself as anything but a loyal American, grateful for his friendships, freedoms and opportunities. Bob found this very surprising, so he asked the question again. He received the same response. Jon did not think of himself as a "victim"; he was utterly sincere in letting go and moving on. This sort of forgiveness can come only through humility, with gratefulness and love.

In the 1980's, JonSons Markets in East Los Angeles was one of my most valued customers. During my regular sales calls to the main office, I was fortunate to meet and talk with Jon on several occasions. He was unaware that I had been told his story, but I knew I was in the presence of a very special man. Forgiveness and reconciliation truly are matters of the heart.

A network of mutuality

It is an important calling to strive to reverse the dreadful impact of Cain's mournful separation from his brother. Martin Luther King climbed to the top of a high mountain peak, where he saw more clearly than anyone else that brothers and sisters of every culture, race, ethnicity and religious faith are inextricably bound in the struggle for harmony within our human family. Here is a profoundly insightful statement from one of his speeches:

> In a real sense all life is inter-related. All men are caught in an inescapable network of mutuality, tied in a single garment of destiny. Whatever affects one directly affects all indirectly. *I can never be what I ought to be until you are what you ought to be. And you can never be what you ought to be until I am what I ought to be.* This is the inter-related structure of reality.[15]

King's "network of mutuality" presents us with a vision of what is possible if we caringly seek out our brother or sister before the next bad thing happens. In working on the BEFORE side of the model above—being proactive—we will surely achieve more in the long run

---

[15] King, *Strength to Love*, ix.

than by being mainly reactive. Our situation calls for a different approach, which necessarily begins with empathy and understanding. The best way to begin to understand another man is to sit down with him and listen to his story, without agenda or judgment. The surest way to earn a man's trust is to become vulnerable and tell him of your own painful journey. Offer your story as a gift without motive, save the hope that you can again be brothers.

One of the clearest examples of how this works is demonstrated in the unlikely relationship between Jackie Robinson and Branch Rickey, the innovative general manager of the Brooklyn Dodgers. Professional baseball had an unwritten rule, preventing men of color from playing in the major leagues. No owner had the courage to break this "color barrier," until Rickey convinced the board of directors to cross the line. In 1945, Robinson signed a contract to play for the Dodgers, a move that created a firestorm of controversy in every corner of the land. Jackie Robinson had superhuman powers of commitment and restraint; few men could match his brand of courage. Fortunately, Branch Rickey was cut from the same cloth of fearlessness and integrity. When these two men swung open the floodgates, many others were able to follow in the rushing currents of opportunity. Jackie Robinson became everything he could be because Branch Rickey was all he could be; Branch Rickey became all he could be because he had a man like Jackie Robinson in his life. This kind of teamwork helps us to remember who our brother is.

> *"Who is your brother?"*

8

GETTING THERE FROM HERE

"There is joy in the presence of the angels of God over one sinner who repents."
GOSPEL OF LUKE

Some time ago, we became lost while on a driving trip through the scenic rural countryside of eastern New York State. We came to a tiny town, which didn't appear on our map. It was noontime, so we stopped to get directions and have lunch at a well-worn roadside diner. Evidently the town didn't get many tourists, because when we entered the place we were greeted with looks of concerned curiosity by a room full of local patrons. When we asked the man behind the counter for directions to Albany, he explained in a serious tone, "I don't think you can get there from here." Really, he did, and he wasn't kidding! He then turned to ask an old timer who was sitting at the lunch counter if he knew the way. In a discouraging tone of voice, the second man replied, "Nope. I've never been out of the county in my life. Sorry, can't help you." We eventually found the road home and had a few laughs along the way. It turns out that Albany was a mere seventeen miles from the nameless town.

The road to forgiven-ness can be like the road to Albany. Some folks simply have no idea how to get there, even if they have lived their entire life just a short distance away.

The trail map

Throughout the preceding pages, we have tried to show that there is a reliable trail map for finding meaning in your life and being at peace with the world.

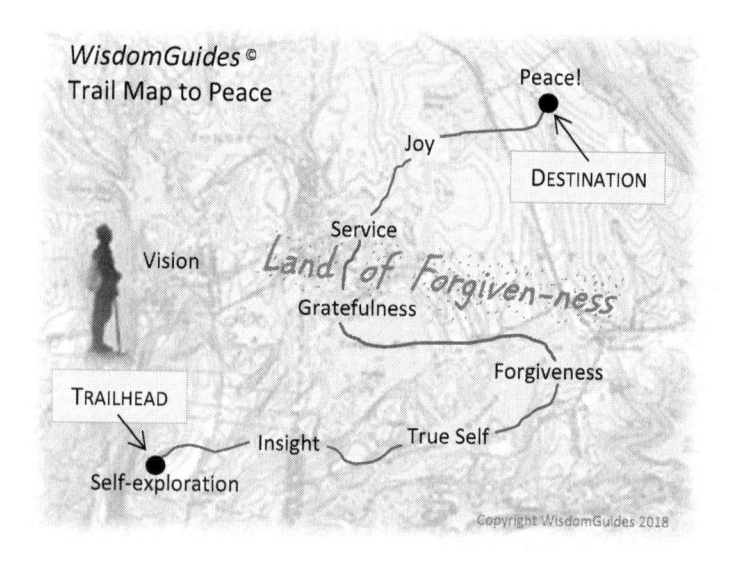

Figure 4

Your journey necessarily begins with the vision you have for a better future. Unless you look beyond your circumstances and see that you have more yet to contribute to a hungry world, you will fall short of your God-given potential. The stark realization that your life is not about you will help guide you to your trailhead.

Self-exploration is the stepping off point that invariably leads to insight into your unique personhood, your True Self. As we discussed in Chapter Three, the discovery of your True Self is a major achievement and is tantamount to personal forgiveness. From that point, it is not difficult to walk toward gratefulness and then find your calling in the world. This calling is never self-serving; rather, it is the clarion's call for you to use your Gifts to benefit humanity.

As we have said before, the highest goal of your life is to find your joy and be at peace. Trappist monk Thomas Merton tells us:

> There is only one problem on which all my existence, my peace and my happiness depend: to discover myself in discovering God. If I find him, I will find myself and if I find my True Self I will find Him.[1]

Could the meaning of your existence be reduced to something as simple as Merton proposes? Will the key to solving the riddle of your life really be found in the discovery of your True Self? How will you know when you have found yourself? No one can answer these questions for you. You must find them out in your own time and in your own way.

Gifts of grace

It is time to affirm one of our most fervently held beliefs: *No one will be truly happy until they make a rigorous self-examination at the spiritual level of*

---

[1] Merton, *Seeds of Contemplation*, 29.

consciousness. This examination is one of the requisites for finding your calling in life and in ultimately leading a life that matters. Hopefully, in the forthcoming pages you will find an entry point for your own introspective assessment.

The Declaration of Independence, written in 1776 by a thirty-three year old patriot, is undoubtedly the most remarkable document of its kind ever written. The Preamble begins with these words, "We hold these Truths to be self-evident, that all men are created equal, that they are endowed by their Creator with certain unalienable Rights, that among these are Life, Liberty and the Pursuit of Happiness."[2] We would like to add the following sentence to Thomas Jefferson's exceptional achievement: "Each human being is created with some measure of aptitude and potential in certain areas of endeavor." These innate endowments can be nurtured to enable a person to achieve success and notoriety. For example, someone who rehearses for thousands of hours on the piano may rise to become a concert pianist. The high school debater with persuasive communication skills may one day become a prominent lawyer or politician. Through effort and determination, a talented athlete might be drafted and make his way to the professional ranks.

Beyond our inherent mental and physical abilities there lies another dimension of personal endowment called "Gifts of the Spirit," which are given by Grace to every human being. These Gifts are discoverable through the practices of silence, prayer and contemplation. We believe that, unlike our temporal endowments, spiritual Gifts remain with us for all eternity.

---

[2] All men are created as equals, but life is inherently unfair. So, the fact that God gave humans the rights to life, liberty and the pursuit of happiness does not guarantee that everyone will be able to exercise those rights. Equality almost never works out in real life. So, who do we blame for that?

People with these Gifts are:

- *Teachers*—men and women who instruct others in the deeper meaning and purpose of life. (e.g., Jesus Christ, Buddha, Thomas Merton)

- *Encouragers*—those who support and sustain others as they seek the path to joy and peace. (e.g., Bill Doulos, Bill W. and Bob S.)

- *Wisemen*—those who have made the great journey of self-discovery, and who faithfully show others the way. They are often mystics and contemplatives. (e.g., Richard Rohr, the Desert Fathers and Mothers, Joseph Campbell)

- *Prophets*—those whose vision of the future is informed by Grace. (e.g., John the Baptist, Rev. Martin Luther King, Nelson Mandela)

- *Leaders*—men and women who have the passion and talents to enable others to fulfill their unique "giftedness." (Abraham Lincoln, Moses, Paul of Tarsus)

- *The Merciful*—people who have compassion and show kindness to those who suffer. (e.g., Frank Buchman, Dorothy Day, William Wilberforce, Gandhi)

- *Healers*—those who help others to remedy the "hole in their soul." (e.g., Fr. Greg Boyle, Rev. Chip Murray, Mother Teresa, Dr. Albert Schweitzer)

- *The Blessed*—this is a special calling reserved for mature persons who have the gift of time. They bless people (especially children) simply by being there with them as they prepare to face the journey ahead. They are fully out of the ego stage of life and are looking to give back and transform the world. (e.g., Thomas Keating, the Dalai Lama, Teresa of Avila, Francis of Assisi)

- *Servers*—those who have discovered the real reason why they are here and are hard at work in the world. (Everyone mentioned in this section of the book)

- *Other Gifts*—this is not an exhaustive list of Gifts of the Spirit. Others like *Generosity* and *Hospitality* encourage social interdependency and build trust within the human family.

It is crucial that each person be aware of and get comfortable with their proportion of God-given Gifts. People who are willing to investigate them and adopt a service mentality will surely find their Joy. We count Joy as the highest form of happiness, which is the gateway to Peace and can be realized only at a spiritual level.

If the idea of Gifts appears to you to be unrelated to forgiveness, we ask you to go deeper. Ask yourself if you are holding something back that would make things better for someone else. Then consider just how much you are willing to risk in forgiving yourself. . . and then in *giving* yourself. *After all, what is your life for if not "for giving"?*

Our story

The *WisdomGuides*© story tells of two men who serendipitously discovered the opportunity to exercise their Gifts in ways that benefit both themselves and others. It began two decades ago, when Tom and I participated in a Gifts workshop that helped us identify what we really have to offer in service to the world. Determining that our Gifts are as Teachers and Encouragers, we began a lengthy period of discernment. We sought out wise men and women—educators, writers, mentors and friends—who helped us find the ideal compass point to follow. Among them was Gordon T. Smith, whose

Courage and Calling, Embracing Your God-Given Potential made a particularly deep impression on us. Through his writings, Smith introduced us to the idea of "vocational integrity," noting, "To live in truth, we must be true to who we are. But this is not possible unless we *know* who we are: how God has made us, how we are unique, how God has made us to serve him in the church and in the world."[3] It just seemed like the right thing to do when we launched *WisdomGuides©* in 2014. We now meet regularly with a Cadre of young men in their late thirties and forties, who contract with us to read, reflect and journal about what is happening in their lives. The selection process is difficult, but thus far just the right mix of men has come our way. We host structured meetings where we break bread, socialize and respond to "wisdom readings," literature by thinkers who bring out our innermost thoughts and feelings. The goal of our Cadre Adventures is to prepare men in the first half of their life for the service they will be called to in the second half, that time of life when they will discover why they are here.

If you are new to the notion of Gifts, it might be helpful to use the following analogy. Let's say you are planning an extended trek through the Sierra Nevada Mountains with a group of backpackers, some who are veterans and others who are novices. Since you are limited by the weight you can carry in your pack, you have to be judicious about what you take along. A seasoned mountaineer wouldn't think of heading into the woods without a map and a compass, but would never pack ceramic dishes or heavy pots and pans. Visualize the backpack as the "container of your life," which holds your best talents, capabilities and creative energies. Whether you are aware of it or not, you are

---

[3] Gordon T. Smith, *Courage and Calling, Embracing Your God-Given Potential* (Downers Grove, IL: Inter-Varsity Press, 1999), 37. Much of this section is attributable to Smith and his influence on the authors.

also packing your Gifts of the Spirit. But they are not in the pack; they are in your soul. If you are an Encourager, you build confidence in the first time backpacker and give him positive assurances when he meets obstacles along the trail. If you possess the Gift of Hospitality, you pitch the tent, start a campfire and then cook a dinner that no one will ever forget. At the end of the day, if you are a Teacher, you point out the constellations and tell tales of long ago journeys into the wild.

The sooner you recognize what your Gifts are and start using them in the way of the backpacker, the better your journey will be. You will begin to get more out of life because you will be putting your energy into your strengths. Here is the story of someone who recognized his Gifts early on, but then wandered off the trail and became hopelessly lost.

The servant

Bill is one of the kindest, gentlest men we know. He was just a kid when he realized he was called to the ministry, so he set the vector of his life in the direction of service. In 1973, Bill got involved with *Koinonia*, a Christian fellowship that emphasizes community and helping others. He subsequently changed his surname from Lane to Doulos as an outward representation of his vocation among the needy. In ancient Greece, the name Doulos meant "one who serves."

Through his church, Bill began working in soup kitchens and outreach ministries to homeless people in the Los Angeles area. Seeing the pathetic condition of so many men and women who were addicted to drugs and alcohol, Bill decided he had to do something more. Fate smiled on him when he acquired a house, which he converted into a sober living home for addicts. Within a few years, Bill's name was listed on nine

"Jubilee Homes," which became places of hope for dozens of destitute people. Bill Doulos knew that he was serving the Lord in a very big way, but what he didn't know was that he was setting himself up for a monumental collapse.

Bill says he felt the need to be rewarded for his loyal service to humanity, so he began smoking *methamphetamine*. The drug made him happy and energetic; it was a great feeling. He used it only occasionally at first, but meth soon became the center of his life. Bill became more reclusive and detached, sometimes losing days at a time while he hid out in his dark apartment. His life was spinning out of control. He began missing meetings and deadlines, lying to people about where he was and what he was doing. He didn't make the mortgage payments on time and the bank foreclosed on one of his homes. By the time his keepers stepped between him and his addiction, Bill was about to lose everything he had worked so hard to get.

Several of his friends staged an intervention and they were able to convince him to enter a detox center in Arizona. After a few weeks he appeared to be well on the road to recovery, but was still using drugs. Then, Bill received a call from a gifted clergyman with a knack for helping lost souls find their way back from the dark side. Like the prodigal's father, he and his wife embraced Bill and showed him a way to set his life back on course. With their encouragement, he soon permanently quit using drugs and alcohol. Jubilee Homes was restructured and the remaining eight homes were consolidated into four. Jubilee was brought under church control and Bill was hired to manage operations. A few years ago, Bill the Servant was ordained by the bishop as a Deacon in the Episcopal Church. Since 2000, more than fifteen hundred people have been through Jubilee's programs for sobriety. With an estimated recidivism rate of about a third, it is estimated that Bill and his dedicated staff have rescued more than a thousand men and women from the annihilation of spirit that addiction brings. Only God knows how many of these people would have ended their lives had they not come in contact with the extraordinary people who work at Jubilee Homes.

When we sat down to talk about his journey through the valley of the shadow of death, I knew only bits and pieces about Bill's life. When I heard the "rest of his story," I was not surprised to find out how he found the path to forgiven-ness. Bill followed the very same recipe for forgiveness that we outline in this book. First, he implored God for mercy and received a clear, affirmative response. He then meticulously traced each one of Alcoholic Anonymous' Twelve Steps and made a thoroughgoing personal inventory. Bill came to accept who he was and forgave himself for making such a mess of his life. When he got to the ninth step (making amends), he did something that is really out of the ordinary. He opened up his address book and sent a letter of confession with a plea for forgiveness to everyone he knew, altogether more than twelve hundred people. In part, Bill's letter read:

> I don't know anyone who sets out in life to become an addict. But one morning recently I woke up and realized that I had become one. In a way you shouldn't have to apologize for an illness. But in another way my recent experience has involved behavioral mistakes that range from poor judgement to hypocrisy, and I do apologize to you for these.[4]

If you are having trouble finding a good example of vulnerability, this would be it. Not everyone found it in their heart to accept Bill's apology; some people still

---

[4] Excerpted from an open letter written by Bill Doulos in Spring 2002.

avoid him like he has the plague. Nevertheless, he has now been fully liberated from the prison of his addiction and found the peace that comes through selfless service to his brothers and sisters. Bill advises, "See yourself as being a servant and you will find refreshment for your soul, and transformation for your life."

Living with regret

Like Bill, almost every one of us has regrets about things that have happened, or could have happened if only we had taken a different approach at times of choice. It would have been better for you to keep quiet instead of berating the brash young clerk behind the service desk. You should have called your sister months ago to apologize for your recent behavior toward her. You feel guilty for not having visited an old friend who suddenly passed away at the retirement home. Life presents us with plenty of opportunities to be regretful.

For many years Bronnie Ware worked as a palliative care nurse for people who were dying. She asked them about regrets they had as they faced their final obstacle on the trail of life. In her words, here is what Ware heard repeated over and over again:

> 1. *I wish I'd had the courage to live a life true to myself, not the life others expected of me.* "This was the most common regret of all. When people realize that their life is almost over and look back clearly on it, it is easy to see how many dreams have gone unfulfilled. Most people had not honored even a half of their dreams and had to die knowing that it was due to choices they had made, or not made. Health

brings a freedom very few realize, until they no longer have it."

2. *I wish I hadn't worked so hard.* "This came from every male patient that I nursed. They missed their children's youth and their partner's companionship. Women also spoke of this regret, but as most were from an older generation, many of the female patients had not been breadwinners. All of the men I nursed deeply regretted spending so much of their lives on the treadmill of a work existence."

3. *I wish I'd had the courage to express my feelings.* "Many people suppressed their feelings in order to keep peace with others. As a result, they settled for a mediocre existence and never became who they were truly capable of becoming. Many developed illnesses relating to the bitterness and resentment they carried as a result."

4. *I wish I had stayed in touch with my friends.* "Often they would not truly realize the full benefits of old friends until their dying weeks and it was not always possible to track them down. Many had become so caught up in their own lives that they had let golden friendships slip by over the years. There were many deep regrets about not giving friendships the time and effort that they deserved. Everyone misses their friends when they are dying."

5. *I wish that I had let myself be happier.* "This is a surprisingly common one. Many did not realize until the end that happiness is a choice. They had stayed stuck in old patterns and habits. The so-called 'comfort' of familiarity overflowed into their emotions, as well as their physical lives. Fear of change had them pretending to others, and to their selves, that

they were content, when deep within, they longed to laugh properly and have silliness in their life again."

No one really wishes to die with personal business left unresolved, but for many of us the pain of change seems overwhelming. Each of these five regrets has something to teach us about finding peace in our lives through the act of forgiveness, particularly through self-forgiveness.[5]

Living with integrity

As Ware reveals, the most common regret of dying people is they wish they had followed their own hopes and dreams, rather than what others expected of them. This is a perfect illustration of the power of the false self in leading us away from who we were meant to be. But in taking a final accounting of their lives, Ware's patients were faced with the possibility of self-forgiveness. While they may have missed their chances earlier, here was one last momentous opportunity to be grateful with what went right with their lives. As we already know, many of these dying people never found their place of peace in the land of forgiven-ness. There are no mulligans in the game of life, so it is wise to take counsel from the dying. "Have courage. Be true to who you are. Set your own expectations and life's goals. Live with integrity." Living with integrity means that what you do matches who you are, that your actions are congruent with your values. When you develop rich

---

[5] Bronnie Ware, *The Huffington Post*, "Top 5 Regrets of the Dying," http://www.huffingtonpost.com/bronnie-ware/top-5-regrets-of-the-dyin_b_1220965.html, (March 2, 2013). Excerpted from: Bronnie Ware, *The Top Five Regrets of the Dying, A Life Transformed by the Dearly Departing* (Carlsbad, CA: Hay House, Inc., 2011–12).

relationships with good people, pursue the right career and give back to the world in ways that feed your spirit, you will not have to ask yourself, "I wish I had. . . . ."

Work in perspective

Based on Gallup© data from its 2013 and 2014 Work and Education polls, nearly forty percent of Americans spend at least fifty hours a week at the office.[6] Nevertheless, the current generation works less and has more leisure time than any of our predecessors. Why then do so many people complain about the pervasiveness of work and the struggle to balance their careers with personal time? Why are so many men and women unhappy in their chosen professions? Perhaps this is so because we are not very good at placing the activity of work into perspective. Work is a necessary and a noble calling. We are created to work and be rewarded by our labors, but when work dominates our attention the way it so often does, it draws us away from what is truly important. Consider that nearly everyone now carries a cell phone with them everywhere they go. It is hard to escape this ubiquitous little device, which links us to business contacts, pings us with text messages and reminds us of impending appointments with bells and whistles. Note how many people fidget as they place their cell phones on the dinner table, so as not to miss a call from the boss or a client. The cell phone can become like a jealous paramour, beckoning us to return to her embrace.

Each summer we vacation at our rustic little Canadian cottage, far removed from the hustle and

---

[6] Lydia Saad, *Gallup News*, "The '40-Hour' Workweek is Actually Longer—by Seven Hours," http://www.gallup.com/poll/175286/hour-workweek-actually-longer-seven-hours.aspx, (April 7, 2016).

bustle of the suburbs. For sixty years, we have managed to survive without modern conveniences like the telephone, television set or even a microwave oven. Recently, we fretted over whether or not to have phone and Internet services installed. After much discussion, our family unanimously agreed that digital services would violate the sacredness of our wilderness space. So, for the time being anyway, it remains difficult to bring the office along on vacation. It usually takes a few days before we fully disengage from the work mindset, but soon we don't miss our favorite cable TV program or the disruptive ding-ding of our cell phones. No one ever expresses regret at having to give up their desktop computer for the gentle simplicity of cottage life.

Finding the delicate balance between work and leisure helps eliminate feelings of regret that might surface later in life. Having to forgive yourself for selfishly spending too much time away from family and friends is not a pleasing prospect.

Truth telling

Bronnie Ware notes that many of her patients regretted not having expressed their true feelings to other people. There is an element of risk in being honest with others and straight talk will not always be rewarded with a better situation. Some of us lack fortitude and skillfulness in expressing ourselves in moments of conflict, which predictably leads to ill feelings about ourselves later on. Nowhere is the art of self-forgiveness more requisite than in cases where we wish we would have said, "Let me tell you how that comment made me feel," or "Your actions were inappropriate, and let me explain why."

Choosing the right time to have a difficult conversation is an acquired skill. Interventions with alcoholics and drug addicts, for example, often fail because the subject is simply not ready to hear the message. Sometimes your best response to something hurtful will be, "I would like to talk with you about what just happened. This is not the time or place, so let's talk about it tomorrow morning." This will give you time to choose your words carefully, while letting the other person know that you are not letting them off the hook. This approach also helps by reducing the level of emotion you feel in the immediate aftermath of something hurtful.

One of our favorite counseling theorems is this: *"There are times when we are called to comfort the afflicted; and times to afflict the comfortable."*[7] Whereas comforting people in distress comes naturally for most of us, afflicting the comfortable can get really dicey. Remember Scott, who saw pridefulness in others, but was shocked to learn about his own overblown ego? By building a bond of trust and candor with Scott, I increased the chances that his response would be a positive one. Had he not been open to the possibility of change, my approach might easily have derailed. Our advice is simple, if not always easy. Speak the truth with sincerity and clarity at the right moment and you will not live to regret it.

Friendships

As we age, "golden friendships" cultivated over many decades become greater and greater treasures. When our children grow up, they often move away to start

---

[7] This expression has been attributed to American journalist Finley Peter Dunne (1867–1936), who used it to describe the crucial role that newspapers play in society. It has been widely used by writers and theologians to affirm Biblical teachings. See: *Dictionary of Christianese*, https://www.dictionaryofchristianese.com/god-comforts-the-afflicted-and-afflicts-the-comfortable/, (May 14, 2018).

their own careers and families, leaving less and less time for them to spend with their parents. While many older folks are fortunate to have time with their grandchildren, much of their socialization necessarily happens with their contemporaries. Retired people are graced by the gift of time, making it easier to write a note or make a phone call to an old friend. However, not everyone takes advantage of these opportunities and they come to regret it later on, especially when someone who has been part of their lives is no longer around.

Ware observes that many people don't realize until it is too late that happiness is an elective in the school of life. Imagine what it must be like to arrive at the very end of your long journey and discover that your life would have been much better if only you had not put so many conditions on your happiness. It must be a terrible feeling to say to yourself, "If only I had patched things up with Aunt Susie before she died," or, "I wish I had gone to my granddaughter's wedding, instead of being angry at her for marrying Mike." Left alone, unfinished business like this can morph into self-pity and shamefulness.

Some of us are naturally happy people, who make everyone around them feel better. My best friend is like this. I have lost count of the people who have told me what a difference her joyful attitude makes. She doesn't dwell on the negative; rather, she says and does things to lift other people's spirits and brighten their days. She never misses a chance to send a birthday card or celebrate a special occasion with the people she knows. She doesn't try to relive the past, focusing instead on the positive side of every situation, no matter what. She makes a habit of looking past people's flaws to find the best in everyone she comes in contact with. People like her will never wish they had chosen to be happier, nor will they have to face the regret of losing touch with old friends.

Regret and forgiveness

It is hard to accept the notion that anyone really wishes to die with loose threads of regret dangling from the tapestry of their lives. You will never hear a young person declare, "I hope to live a life marked by unhappiness and regret!" What then contributes to regretfulness in older persons? We can only surmise that certain people become so conditioned by their difficult circumstances that they develop a sense of unworthiness; they become convinced that they deserve to be unhappy. These folks make the choice to stay bogged down in the quagmire of their laments, making it more and more difficult to confront the truth and make those changes necessary for them to be happier. This rang clear to me in a conversation with a good friend, who shared with me how unhappy her aged mother is; how she feels victimized by her "hard life." She complains about everything and is in complete denial of her unhappiness. My friend said she cannot remember the last time she saw her mother smile, much less laugh. With her time winding down, she has lost her willingness to let loose and have a little fun. Why do we allow this to happen to us?

Neuroscience only recently discovered that the brain has a clear *negativity bias*, causing stronger emotional reactions to negative events than to positive ones.

> The brain prefers to constellate around fearful, negative, or problematic situations. In fact, when a loving, positive, or unproblematic thing comes your way, you have to savor it consciously for at least fifteen seconds before it can harbor and store itself in your "implicit memory;" otherwise it doesn't stick. We must indeed savor the good in order to significantly change our regular attitudes and moods. And

we need to strictly monitor all the "Velcro" negative thoughts.[8]

If researchers are correct, we might conclude that it is easier to be a negative person than a positive one. Perhaps we humans are prone to judgment rather than empathy and understanding, to indictment rather than tolerance, to blame without personal accountability. Our negativity bias feeds directly into pride and ego, making it more difficult to seek forgiveness and reconciliation with other people.[9]

Self-assessment questions

No matter what your age or what your story, today is a good time to begin eliminating the conditions in your life that lead to regretfulness. Let's review your responses to the questions we posed at the end of Chapter Three. Here are the questions again:

1. How would you describe your relationship with your father? Your mother?

2. Is there anything they could have done differently to make your life better?

3. If you could change one thing about your spouse/significant other, what would that be?

---

[8] Richard Rohr, Center for Action and Contemplation, "Turning Toward the Good," https://cac.org/turning-toward-the-good-2016-02-18/, (February 18, 2016).

[9] Additional information on the brain's negativity bias can be found in an article by Hara Estroff Marano, *Psychology Today*, "Our Brain's Negative Bias," https://www.psychologytoday.com/articles/200306/our-brains-negative-bias. (June 20, 2003). See also: Tony Schwartz, *New York Times*, "Overcoming Your Negativity Bias," http://dealbook.nytimes.com/2013/06/14/overcoming-your-negativity-bias/?_r=0, (June 24, 2016).

4. Has someone you care about tried to hurt you and not earnestly apologized?

5. Has something happened to you that has caused you to feel like a victim?

Coming to terms with our personal history naturally forces us to consider the conditions of our youth. Most people have at least some criticism of their parents or someone else who helped to raise them. Those who were orphaned or abandoned have a particularly difficult time in addressing their upbringing. Abuse, addiction and loneliness characterize the childhoods of many who never experienced the love and affection they so desperately longed for. Pardoning a mother or father for unintended errors in parental judgment is easy compared to the effort it takes to forgive an addictive mother who never seemed to care about you. How easy is it to find forgiveness in your heart for your biological father whom you never met because he left your mother to fend for herself before you were born? In these extreme cases, only your Higher Power can lead you to forgiven-ness.

If your upbringing was somewhat "normal," i.e. absent the extreme, be thankful that your parents or guardians at least tried to do right by you. If you are grateful to your parents, count yourself among the lucky ones. Conversely, if you have unfinished business with the people who hurt you when you were young and vulnerable, the following is for you. Holding onto bitterness and regret is not going to make your life better or make you happier. Your mother and father are/were human beings with their share of flaws and shortcomings. They may not have been equipped to handle the job of a parent in the way they should have. They were bound to fail at times—perhaps often—in their parental roles and their failures caused you pain and suffering. Even if they had it to do over, they might screw things up again. If you have children of your own, it is fair to ask yourself (gain insight into) how you are doing as a parent. What are you doing differently than your parents did to ensure that your kids have the best childhood possible? We are not talking here about making sure they have plenty of activities to fill up the calendar hanging on the refrigerator door. We are not talking about signing up your son for baseball, enrolling your daughter in music lessons, or taking the family to the amusement park. We are talking about your efforts at clear communication with your kids, about spending individual time with them to discover who they are and what they are interested in. We are talking about encouraging your children to express their feelings without fear of judgment and about teaching them honesty and integrity. We are talking about sharing yourself in intimate and nurturing ways, so that your kids know how much you love them.

Let's be real! You're not going back to your childhood, except in your memory. Your mom and dad will have to make their own accounting of things that happened, or should have happened. Now is the time for you to forgive your parents and let it go. The poison of resentment and regret is killing you, not them!

Where is forgiveness called for in your current relationships? Is there something about your spouse or partner that you absolutely deplore? Perhaps your wife did something that was uncalled for and you are still stewing about it. But before you continue to see her as "the impudent offender," consider what part you may have played in the incident. You may find nothing to implicate yourself, but it is both necessary and revealing to examine your intentions, your words and your actions. The part you "own" may simply be your response to what happened.

Suppose you find out that your husband had an affair with a woman he met at the office. Whether he is ready to admit it or not, he is accountable both to you and to

God for his misdeeds. But how can you forgive a man in whom you put your complete trust, and who then betrayed you in such a hurtful manner? As you seek answers to why he did what he did, you admit that for months communication with your husband had been breaking down. You were deeply troubled by the lack of intimacy between you and you did not recall the last time you made love. You argued with your husband and you said a few things to him that you wish you hadn't. You thought about asking your husband to go to counseling, but feared that he might react badly, so you kept quiet.

Do *you* also stand in need of forgiveness for any part you played in this drama? At the risk of sounding like a victim blamer, the answer is an unequivocal. . . "Maybe, and probably yes!" It is very clear that you are in no way responsible for your husband's wrongdoing and your decision not to suggest counseling was made in good faith, so please don't regret it. But don't wait any longer in demanding that your husband seek professional help. In most cases you will do best by attending counseling together.

The angry words you used when you found out about the affair are part of the normal human response when someone breaks a trust and undermines a relationship. Your anger was probably good therapy for you in that moment. But afterwards (remember, you also said some hurtful things *before* you found out), did you do and say things to deliberately hurt your husband? Did you move from reaction to retaliation? If you answered "yes" to these questions, then you are in need forgiveness, too. Let me repeat, you don't need forgiveness for what your husband did to jeopardize your marriage. That regrettable choice was his, and his alone! However, you must take full responsibility for words and actions designed to make him "pay" for his infidelity. If he wants to reconcile with you, your husband will have to make restitution by a sincere, heartfelt apology and by taking concrete steps to permanently change his behavior. If you want to save your marriage and rebuild your relationship, then you will have to admit where *you* crossed the line.

There is another aspect of your relationship that you might want to think about. The best marriages are those built on mutual trust and intimacy. When these components are missing it is a red flag that something is wrong. Try to discover what that something is and commit yourself to restoring the love and affection you had when you were happiest together.

The big forgiveness

We have grappled with some very difficult concepts throughout the preceding pages and readily concede that forgiven-ness is a hard place to come to. Forgiving others is a commonplace occurrence, but self-forgiveness is unexplored territory for many (if not most) of us. There are few road maps to get us there and reliable guides always seem in short supply.

We have stressed the importance of getting back into right relationship with God and with our fellow travelers on the trail of life. We will likely never be "all square" with every person we know, but God is always open to a full reconciliation. No matter how another human being responds to our attempts at forgiveness, we can always count on our Higher Power to unconditionally accept our humble admissions of wrongdoing and our pleas for mercy. The "peace that passes all understanding" can be gained through Him, even after everyone else has rejected us.

Back in Chapter Six, we introduced Reinhold Niebuhr's paradoxical description of what he termed "the impossible possibility." The greatest forgiver of all once assured us, "What is impossible with man is possible with God."[10] The impossible *is* possible; the unforgivable *can* be forgiven. Niebuhr authored the well-known "Serenity Prayer," which gives us a generous entrée into the space of self-forgiveness. In its simplest form, it reads like this:

> God, grant me the serenity to accept the
>   things I cannot change,
> Courage to change the things I can,
> And wisdom to know the difference.

One does not have to be a theologian to recognize that some things, no matter how hard we try, are simply beyond our control. There is a serenity that comes from knowing and embracing our limitations, letting go of our manipulating false self in favor of our deeper, truer nature. Tom calls this, "moving from ego to Grace."

Courage is the indispensable quality, the single most valuable asset a person can possess in seeking the purpose for their life. Embedded in the word "encourage," it drowns out the voices of doubt and inspires us to get moving. We *can* choose to change what's wrong with our situation and courage allows us to do this. So, pray then that you gain wisdom in discerning what you can fix and what you cannot.

When I consider the greatheartedness it must take to forgive the unforgiveable, I see the placid face of Corrie ten Boom. During World War II, her family's home in Haarlem, Holland, became a "safe house" for refugees fleeing Nazi oppression. Owing to the ten Boom's activism in the Dutch underground movement, hundreds of Jews, Christians and other enemies of the Gestapo made their way to freedom. But in February 1944, they were betrayed and several family members, including Corrie, were sent to Ravensbruck Camp near Berlin, Germany. When the war ended fifteen months

---

[10] Luke, 18:27.

later, Corrie returned home and committed the rest of her life to a ministry of reconciliation. She testified to the liberating power of forgiveness, saying: "There is no pit so deep that God's love is not deeper still. God will give us the love to be able to forgive our enemies." Ironically, though she had been tortured and humiliated on a daily basis in a Nazi concentration camp, she had yet to face her biggest test.

In the 1970s, when she told her compelling story in the best-selling book *The Hiding Place*, Corrie ten Boom became an internationally recognized figure. She addressed audiences around the world, appealing to people everywhere to heed the teachings of Christ and forgive one another, no matter how grave the offense. One day after one of her talks, a man who had been seated in the crowd approached her. He tremulously extended his hand and asked her to forgive him for the awful things he had done to her. It was then that she recognized him as one of the men who had beaten her at Ravensbruck. At first, repulsed by bitter memories from her past, she could not bring herself to touch him. But then she did something that marked her as authentic. She emotionally took his hand in hers and she forgave him. In that moment, one incredibly courageous woman was finally released from the prison walls that held her captive in her deep interior, in the wilderness of her soul. Corrie ten Boom is witness to what it means to be free, truly free at last![11]

Stories like this demonstrate that the real power of forgiveness is not in withholding it, but in giving it unreservedly to the penitent offender. Martin Luther King had it right when he asserted, "He who is devoid of the power to forgive is devoid of the power to love."

---

[11] Corrie ten Boom House Foundation website, "Home Information History," (September 9, 2016). This powerful story is also told in *Lessons of the Wild*, 90.

The final form of love

Reinhold Niebuhr is one of the "inimitable trailblazers" we alluded to in the beginning of the book. It is fitting that we end our journey together with this pearl of his great wisdom.

> Nothing that is worth doing can be achieved in our lifetime; therefore we must be saved by hope. Nothing which is true or beautiful or good makes complete sense in any immediate context of history; therefore we must be saved by faith. Nothing we do, however virtuous, can be accomplished alone; therefore we must be saved by love. No virtuous act is quite as virtuous from the standpoint of our friend or foe as it is from our standpoint. Therefore we must be saved by the final form of love which is forgiveness.[12]

In the final analysis there is only one kind of forgiveness that is necessary for a happy life. Forgiveness is a profoundly personal matter. It begins and ends when you open your heart and ask for mercy from your Heavenly Father. Your courage to confront the truth will set you free, even when you are unable to forgive another person for what they did to you. God always sees through your brokenness and fills the hole in your soul. Make amends with Him and you will find peace, even unto the end of your days and beyond.

☐

This is not the end!

---

[12] From the writings of Reinhold Niebuhr.

Ask yourself how can you put your energy into something that will make a real difference each day of the rest of your life? Whatever you do, we urge you to keep it simple and stay focused on the ultimate prize. You will find encouragement and be perpetually renewed with hope if you consider pursuing these aims:

1. The knowledge and love of yourself as a unique and extraordinary person

2. The knowledge of your calling in the world and the joy that comes from using your Gifts in the service of others

3. The knowledge and Love of God, where you will find Grace in unexpected abundance

EPILOGUE

We confess that during the writing of this book we wondered if the world needs another book on the topic of forgiveness.[1] Perhaps *The Truth About Forgiveness* was not really a means of helping others, but merely a therapy for our own unfinished business. Personally, I wondered if my lack of credentials in the clinical professions disqualified me from rendering a helpful method of recovery from the pathologies of unforgiveness. Thankfully, whenever we expressed our concerns to friends and colleagues we were urged to continue. Tom and I recalled brief conversations we had with Lew Smedes, whose classic *Forgive and Forget, Healing the Hurts We Don't Deserve* has been in print for a long time and is still widely read. Having finished this book, we now realize that Lew was a big influence on the way it turned out.

Observing how much hurt there is in our world and how many opportunities there are to patch things up, I am persuaded that Tom and I have spent our time well. Surely, there will never be enough forgiveness to fix all that ails humankind, but the stories we hear fill us with hope for a better tomorrow.

My sister Kathy reminded me of the tragic, yet miraculous story of Dan and Lynn Wagner. Their story is tragic because in 2001 their two beautiful daughters, Mandie and Carrie, were killed by a drunk driver in a violent automobile crash in Santa Cruz, California. The girls died at the scene of the accident, and though Dan and Lynn were in critical condition, they eventually made a full recovery. The woman who caused the accident fled the scene with her two infant children, but was soon apprehended. She was tried and

---

[1] An *Amazon*© word search turns up some 14,000 titles and formats, with forgiveness books ranging from the secular to the deeply religious.

convicted of manslaughter, after which she served six and a half years in prison. But there is another side to the Wagner's story and it is the stuff of miracles. In an open letter he calls, "According to His Purpose," here is how Dan tells it:

> Luis Palau held his evangelical festival, Beachfest Santa Cruz, at Main Beach on Saturday and Sunday, Sept. 22 and 23, 2001. Lynn and I and our two teenage girls, Mandie and Carrie, attended the Saturday event, along with about 20,000 other people. Lynn had gone earlier that day to the prayer meeting, and the girls and I caught up with her in the afternoon.
>
> We left Beachfest that evening and headed for our car parked in the neighborhood across from the trestle where we usually park to go to the Boardwalk. We drove up Cayuga St. toward Broadway, heading home to the Live Oak area. A woman who was drunk and had coke and meth in her system had just picked up her two kids from a babysitter, and was driving her Suburban on Windsor St. toward Cayuga at almost fifty miles per hour, ran the stop sign, and crashed into us on the left side of our minivan. The impact sent us into a power pole and then onto a neighbor's front yard.
>
> Neither Lynn nor I have any memories of the accident, and very few memories of that day. Lynn remembers leaving the prayer session before the Saturday festivities began, and hearing God's voice in her heart that it was not the worst thing in the world for a Christian to die. She wasn't sure why God spoke that to her, but she certainly didn't think it was meant for herself.
>
> We woke up in Dominican Hospital, Lynn on Sunday morning and I on Monday morning.

Lynn had three fractured ribs and a broken pelvis in two places that prevented her from putting any weight on one leg for about six weeks. I had no fractures but suffered torn cartilage in my chest, a sprained coccyx (tail bone area), a neck injury, and embedded safety glass in my face and arm that had to be removed later. Both of us had concussions. Lynn remembers that Luis Palau had visited her Sunday morning before going back to Beachfest for the second day; I was still unconscious in the ICU.

My pastor has said that he told me right away when I seemed coherent – I don't remember. The first time I remember grasping it was when someone visiting me in my hospital room had said that they were sorry for my loss. I had asked, "What loss?" They told me I had lost my girls. I remember sharing that news with others who came to visit as if it were a baseball score; it's amazing what shock and medications can do to your emotions.

My Mom and Dad in Oregon were called the night of the accident, and drove down right away. They had a key to our house and let themselves in, cleaned up a bit, and came to the hospital. I remember how comforting it was to see them when my bed was wheeled into the room Lynn was already in. My Dad told me the first thing he had done when he saw me in the ICU was reach for my legs to see if they were still there. I remember also how good it felt to finally take a shower, which was located across the hall from our recovery room. As I walked back in my robe toward our room, I saw a lady writing on the butcher paper the staff had taped to our door—apparently we were attracting too many visitors, so they were being asked to write notes on the butcher paper instead. The lady turned around and saw me reading what she was writing. I gave her a big hug and invited her in to see Lynn. Robyn now has her own story to tell of what God has done through this accident.

I was discharged to go home on Thursday but Lynn was sent to the Recovery Care Unit, located in the former Santa Cruz Community Hospital building where both Mandie and Carrie were born. She spent about a week and a half there letting her fractures begin to heal.

Our pastor Barney performed an interment service for the girls at Holy Cross Cemetery on Friday, October 12, and a memorial service the following day at Twin Lakes Church in Aptos. At the interment, Barney could not contain his emotions as he spoke what was on his heart. The realization that the pain of losing the girls was not our pain alone, but was shared by everyone who knew and loved them, stunned me. It seemed that everyone we knew came to the memorial service, including the guys I had worked with at a hospital in Salinas. I remember being a little too exuberant when I saw the guys in the hallway before the service began, and later wondered what they thought of me and my apparent lack of grief. All I can say is, it's amazing what shock and medications can do to your emotions.

My Mom and Dad stayed with us for a couple of weeks. I would hear Lynn getting up each morning, and peek down the hall to see her and my Mom hugging and crying. I felt guilty because I wasn't yet suffering with the same grief Lynn was. I can now attribute that to a few things: the pain of my injuries, my narcotic pain meds, and the fact that I was no longer getting up at 5:00 in the morning to go to work all day, but staying home with the one I love. Eventually the pain diminished, I trimmed down on the meds, and the novelty of being home all day wore off. It took about a year; then all hell broke loose inside of me. While Lynn was processing and healing, I was heading off in the opposite direction.

We had been interviewed twice by the Santa Cruz Sentinel newspaper. In one article I was quoted saying, "I feel God's Holy Spirit is resting on me and allowing me to physically heal before I grieve." My time was coming soon.

I guess what triggered my anger and resentment toward God in those days were the Scriptures I kept running into, such as Ephesians 6:2,3 (HCSB): "Honor your father and mother--which is the first commandment with a promise--that it may go well with you and that you may have a long life in the land." Nobody had honored their parents more than Mandie and Carrie had, and yet that promise was not for them – why not? And Psalm 1:6 (HCSB): "For the LORD watches over the way of the righteous..." Psalm 25:13 (HCSB): "and his descendants will inherit the land." Proverbs 12:21 (HCSB): "No disaster overcomes the righteous..." Those didn't apply to us either, so why bother asking God for protection? In fact, why bother asking God for anything? If He couldn't or wouldn't protect my precious girls, how could I trust Him with anything else in my life? Someone had told me it was OK to be angry at God – He's big enough to handle it. But what they didn't say was whether *I* was big enough to handle it. My depression deepened as I grieved the loss of my girls *and* my relationship with God.

Lisa, the woman who hit us, was sentenced to prison the following March for 7 years 8 months. But in my mind, she was a minor player; God was the perpetrator. Consider this example: The four of us are taking a walk, and along a particular section of sidewalk a brick wall begins to rise. One of my daughters steps onto the wall and walks along it as it rises higher and higher, eventually reaching several feet above the sidewalk. A dog suddenly barks right next to her, and she loses her balance and falls toward the sidewalk. I'm standing right there, and could easily catch her if I choose to. I don't. I can perfectly understand my wife's rage at me, not the dog, for letting our daughter fall to the concrete and getting injured, and would be hard pressed to give her a reason for my inaction. These were my thoughts toward God. Why didn't He act to protect us? I was His child and had gone to church all my life. I was a good person and had even served in leadership. I was entitled to His protection, wasn't I?

I had conjured up an image, probably from watching too many war movies, of God as an Army general (like Patton), standing in the map room, drawing up strategies. He points to a particular location on a map and says to one of his colonels, "If we move this platoon into this area and draw the enemy in, then we can move this brigade around the enemy and defeat them there." The colonel replies, "Yes that would work, but you realize that these troops you're moving in will suffer great loss." God says, "Yes, don't worry, I'll take care of that. But I am unwilling to let this opportunity for victory pass." This fantasizing has led me to believe that perhaps God, with the Big Picture in mind, isn't as concerned about our individual suffering and pain level (as we might think) as He is about saving people.

I came to realize that I have a choice of what to believe about God, whether to believe my own thoughts and feelings or to believe the revelation God Himself gave us, that is, the Bible. My own thoughts and feelings want me to believe that perhaps:

1. God did not have the power to stop the accident.
2. God did not know it was going to happen.
3. God was tied up with other business and could not attend to us at that time.
4. God did not have the authority to stop the accident.
5. He simply didn't care.

Or I can choose to believe what He said about Himself in the Bible:

1. He is all-powerful—He could have stopped it.
2. He is all-knowing—He certainly knew it was going to happen.
3. He is everywhere at all times – He was there then.
4. He is sovereign – He had the authority to stop it.
5. He is Love – therefore this action, or non-action, on His part was an expression of His love.

That last part about God's love is the hardest for me to grasp. How could having my girls taken at such a young age be an act of love toward me? I don't know; it's a complete mystery to me. But I must choose either to accept it, or reject everything the Bible tells me about God – there is no picking and choosing what to believe; it's all or nothing. Either the Bible, that is, God's own revelation about Himself, is correct and reliable, or it isn't.

We got a letter in August 2008 from a parole officer that Lisa would be released from prison on September 8 after serving 85% of her sentence, as mandated by the judge. I called the parole officer and asked if he could set up a meeting between Lisa and us so we could finally meet her. I explained that we had never gone to court because she had pleaded guilty, and therefore we had never actually met her. The parole officer said it was an unusual request, and that meeting with us was against Lisa's conditions of parole. Since he didn't have the authority to grant it, he asked me to write a letter stating our case that he could present to his superiors. I did, and heard back that our request had been approved to meet at the Parole Office in Santa Cruz. So we set a date— a date, as it turned out, just a few days shy of the 7th anniversary of the accident.

Lynn and I took along the director of a recovery house in town who had come out of a drug-and-alcohol background and had accepted Jesus. We felt she would be a good person to help us interact, as she had been corresponding with Lisa in prison over the past year. We met the director beforehand to show her the girls' gravesites at Holy Cross Cemetery, then on to the parole office. I'm sure each of us had something we wanted to say or ask of Lisa, but we really didn't discuss it. Personally, I just wanted to get this meeting over with and get that last door closed. We knew from the moment she was sentenced to prison six and a half years earlier that the day would eventually come when we'd meet her, and we wanted that first meeting to be in a controlled environment like this, not in the check-out line at some grocery store.

When the three of us, following behind the parole officer, walked into the meeting room and laid our eyes on Lisa for the first time, it seemed natural for each of us to greet her with a hug; no exception for me. But when I hugged her, I started crying and couldn't stop and couldn't let go. The thought crossed my mind that this may have seemed awkward or unseemly, but in my heart I felt a sense of relief. After seven years, I was finally meeting the woman who had killed my daughters. But I felt no anger, no hatred – just relief. So I cried.

We eventually sat down around a large table. Neither Lynn nor I can remember much about the meeting nor who spoke first, but it was evident that the Holy Spirit was there. We do remember that Lisa talked of her new relationship with Jesus and her 12-step recovery process, and that step 9, Making Amends, would be for her a living amends. Lynn asked her to clarify what she meant by that. Lisa explained that she wanted to share her experience with others and convince them to not do what she had done that took the lives of Mandie and Carrie. She would invest her life, as it were, to make that kind of living amends in the girls' names. I thanked her for pleading guilty and keeping us out of the court proceedings. She kept saying, "I *was* guilty." Then, to wrap up the meeting, the parole officer said that he had never seen anything like this, and it was happening only because of our faith. Then he said that *we* serve a God of reconciliation, including himself in that statement. The three of us walked out of that building rejoicing that the final door had been closed, that the meeting we had dreaded was certainly covered by God's grace, and that even Lisa and her parole officer had professed faith in Him. Lynn and Lisa have since spoken together to various audiences, and have been interviewed by the pastor of a large church here in Santa Cruz County. God continues His marvelous work in people's lives on the issue of forgiveness.

At the time of this writing, it has been nine and a half years since the accident. My relationship with God has been healing, and may even be deeper and more genuine than before; Lynn and I are, separately and together, involved in ministries that, in our "former life," would have been unimaginable. Someone early on had told us that God does not waste His children's pain. God has certainly used us to save and touch many people's lives. It may happen some day in Heaven—for all believers—that lines will form with people telling us that they are there because of our testimonies. Sometimes it's hard for me to rejoice at that prospect while I long to have my girls with me now, but the fact is that in Heaven we'll feel no sorrow or grief, no suffering or pain of loss. While I have considered that I may never again feel a true sense of joy or happiness in this life, I know that when God is done with me here, I will spend eternity with Him and with our girls in Heaven. And then I'll rejoice!

One last thought. Recently I visited a friend in the hospital recovering from a motorcycle accident. The day before, he had had a transmetatarsal amputation of his left foot. As he talked about it he seemed a bit cavalier, and I realized that he was still under heavy medication. I can certainly relate to that. Because he well remembers our girls and the accident, I wanted to tell him: *When you go home and the medications wear off, and you realize the full impact of your loss, don't do what I did. Don't shake your fist at God and demand to know why He didn't protect you. Those were the darkest days of my life. Know that God loves you very much, and cares about your pain and loss. Know also that while He may not restore what you've lost, as you allow Him He will heal you and use you to bring others to Him.*

I do believe that God does not waste our pain. And I know that He sees the Bigger Picture. Pain and suffering are the way of life on Earth, no exceptions. But if our aim is to bring others to Jesus, then how we respond to suffering is so important to those around us who don't yet know Jesus. "You are the light of the world," Jesus said. But if, like my garage flashlight, our light is dim or flickers or keeps turning off by itself, how will they "see your good works and give glory to your Father in heaven?" (Matthew 5:14-16) 1 Peter 2:21 says, "For you were called to this, because Christ also suffered for you, leaving you an example, so that you should follow in His steps." *Amen!*

The Wagners have dedicated themselves to sharing their story with as many people as possible. They have graciously allowed us to use Dan's letter and their compelling video to encourage others in avoiding the terrible fate that befell two families on September 22,

2001.[1] Lynn and Lisa have appeared together to speak about the deadly consequences of driving under the influence of drugs and alcohol. Imagine the impact it makes on an audience when Lynn tells them how violently Mandie and Carrie were taken from her, followed by Lisa who introduces herself as the woman who killed Lynn's children.

I question whether many of us would have the wherewithal to forgive a person who recklessly changed our life forever. Ask yourself if you could come face to face with the "killer," and instead of rebuking her, hug her and weep compassionately together. The Wagners' forgiveness was an unexpected gift to Lisa, the gift of Grace that could have come only from one place.

Yes, the world needs another book on forgiveness, if only to remind us that happiness is a choice and that peace and freedom reign in the land of forgiven-ness!

☐

---

[1] Jamie Rom, Twin Lakes Church, "A Testimony of Forgiveness, Featuring the Wagner Family," https://vimeo.com/162325468, (January 10, 2018). See page 196 for instructions on how to view the Wagner's moving video from your smartphone.

Keys To Forgiveness

Suffering is inevitable, and sadly enough, we seem to bring much of it on ourselves. (ii.)

The desire for happiness is deeply embedded in our DNA, yet it has become tragically elusive for people living in these post-modern times. (iii.)

Forgiveness is the art of letting go in order to find peace in your life. (19.)

The act of forgiveness can sometimes be a one-way street, while reconciliation necessarily requires an affirmative response from the offended persons. (22.)

Forgiveness guidelines: a) If someone indicates that you offended them, whether you meant to or not, tell them you are sorry; b) If you (feel that you) have been offended, tell the offender in a sincere and forthright manner; c) If you think you have offended someone, but are not sure, discuss it with them as soon as possible. (22.)

All behavior is motivated by our desire to enhance and reinforce our self-image. (34.)

All behavior is designed to get us something we want. (109.)

More harm is caused by those who take offense, than by those who give offense. (63.)

We are told there's a hole in the ozone, but we have holes in our souls. (29.)

Every truly happy person we meet who is over fifty is on a spiritual journey. (iii.)

It is possible to be grateful and not happy, but it is impossible to be happy and not grateful. (111.)

Until we connect our outer self with our inner being, we will not live a life of integrity. (110.)

A man cannot get enough of what he does not want. (38.)

The statute of limitations on our pain will eventually run out and then we are best advised to confront what happened. (10.)

No one will be truly happy until they make a rigorous self-examination at the spiritual level of consciousness. (147.)

The place God calls you to is the place where your deep gladness and the world's deep hunger meet. (ii.)

There are times when we are called to comfort the afflicted; and times to afflict the comfortable. (160.)

Everything can be taken from a man but one thing: the last of the human freedoms—to choose one's attitude in any given set of circumstances, to choose one's own way. (24.)

Anything we do that does not bring us together serves to divide us. (79.)

The goal when invited into the drama triangle is not to rescue and not abandon the players who are in conflict. (76.)

He who is devoid of the power to forgive is devoid of the power to love. (131.)

I can never be what I ought to be until you are what you ought to be. And you can never be what you ought to be until I am what I ought to be. (142.)

It takes a vision of something better for people to actually make the choice to move to a happier place in their lives. (35.)

True and lasting forgiveness of any kind can be achieved only after we surrender to a Power greater than us. (47.)

WisdomGuides© Vocabulary

Below is an alphabetical listing of selected terms and expressions used in the book.

afflictive emotions: see footnote, page 30.

double down: this is "power language," for wagering that a firmly held position will prove to be correct or profitable. (30.)

false self: the fake image we create to protect our egos in its dealings with the world; in contrast to our True Self, or authentic person we are at our deepest center. (31.)

get to: see footnote, p. 14.

hooks: see footnote, p. 82.

new see: a previously undiscovered perspective or potential course of action. It happens when a person examines their biases and motivations (insight), or when someone gains an appreciation for another's point of view. (48.)

paradox of insight: although we think we know something by external observation (i.e., from the outside in), wisdom comes from understanding our personal projections from the inside out. (67.)

self-projection: see footnote, p.63.

unfinished business: refers to persistent, undealt with pain caused by a fractured relationship with another person or our Higher Power. (i.)

why bother: indicates there are deeper reasons for expending time and energy in writing a book, or having a conversation with someone in distress. (23.)

Wisdom Books

Title:	Author:
Lessons of the Wild	Edwin L. Andersen
Denial of Death	Ernest Becker
Iron John	Robert Bly
Hero with a Thousand Faces	Joseph Campbell
Pilgrim at Tinker Creek	Annie Dillard
Wild at Heart	John Eldridge
The Prophet	Kahlil Gibran
Invitation to Love	Thomas Keating
Teachings of the Insentient, Zen and the Environment	John Daido Loori
Wisdom of Wilderness	Gerald May
Seeds of Contemplation	Thomas Merton
The Return of the Prodigal Son	Henri J.M. Nouwen
Let Your Life Speak	Parker Palmer
Adam's Return, The Five Promises of Male Initiation	Richard Rohr
Beyond the Postmodern Mind	Huston Smith
The Power of Now	Eckhart Tolle

These books represent a mere sampling of great books that can stir our consciousness toward our deeper self. While these writers are among our favorites, there are many others to be discovered at your local bookstore or via online search engines.

Making a Grateful Box

A "Grateful Box" is a great way to remind yourself and others that you are thankful for all that you have. It is the kind of unique gift that is guaranteed to get a positive response from the recipient. Use any small box like the ones you find at the local discount or home goods store. We use boxes about the size of a recipe box, but the size of the box is not as important as what you put in it. First, print "Grateful Box" on a piece of cardstock and cut it to an appropriate size. Then, using double-sided tape or glue, apply the card to the top of the box. Below is a set of instructions for using the box, which you can customize any way you want.

How to Use Your Grateful Box

Please keep this Grateful Box on your desk or nightstand. When you are grateful to another person, or for something that happens to bless your life, make a note and place it inside. Whenever you are feeling down or sad, open up your Grateful Box and count your blessings. Being grateful for small things adds up to gratefulness, full of grateful... full of Grace! Next holiday season, place the Grateful Box on the Thanksgiving table or under the Christmas tree. When you open it, you will be reminded of how lucky you are to be you. Bless others by giving a Grateful Box to someone you love.

After you print or write the instructions, cut them out and apply them to the inside of the box lid. You can also cut small sheets of blank paper to fit into the box for writing gratitude messages. In lieu of an actual box, some people use social media pages devoted strictly to the Grateful Box idea. Any practice of gratefulness, like the Grateful Box, is sure to brighten up your life and pick you up when you need a lift. It will also lead you toward a place where you will become more forgiving. The Grateful Box really works!

Bibliography

Andersen, Edwin L. *Lessons of the Wild, Learning from the Wisdom of Nature*. Eugene, OR: Wipf & Stock, 2009.

Baldwin, James. *The Fire Next Time*. New York: The Dial Press, 1963.

Becker, Ernest. *The Denial of Death*. New York: The Free Press, 1973.

Bloom, Allen. *The Closing of the American Mind*. New York: Simon and Schuster, 1988.

Boyle, Gregory, S.J. *Tattoos on the Heart, The Power of Boundless Compassion*. New York: Free Press, 2010.

Brown, Brené. *Daring Greatly, How the Courage to Be Vulnerable Transforms the Way We Live, Love, Parent, and Lead*. New York: Gotham Books, 2012.

Buechner, Frederick. *Wishful Thinking, A Seeker's ABC*. New York: HarperOne, 1993.

Coates, Ta-Nehisi. *Between Me and the World*. New York: Random House Books, 2015.

Eldridge, John. *Wild at Heart, The Secret of a Man's Soul*. New York: Thomas Nelson, 2001.

Frankl, Viktor. *Man's Search for Meaning, An Introduction to Logotherapy*. Boston: Beacon Press, 1982.

Haidt, Jonathan. *The Righteous Mind, Why Good People are Divided by Politics and Religion*. New York: Vintage Books, 1912.

Hawkins, David R. *Power vs. Force, The Hidden Determinants of Human Behavior*. Carlsbad, CA: Hay House, Inc., 2002.

Jung, Carl. *Memories, Dreams, Reflections*. New York: Random House, 1989.

Keating, Thomas. *Invitation to Love*. New York: The Continuum Publishing Co., 1995.

Kepler, Thomas S., Ed., *The Journal of John Woolman*. New York: The World Publishing Co., 1954.

King, Jr., Martin Luther. *Strength to Love*. Minneapolis, MN: Fortress Press, 2010.

Lean, Garth. *Frank Buchman, A Life*. London: Constable & Robinson, Ltd., 1985.

Merton, Thomas. *The Seven Storey Mountain*. New York: Harcourt, Brace & Co., 1948.

———. *Seeds of Contemplation*. Norfolk, CN: New Directions Books, 1949.

———. *The Wisdom of the Desert*. New York: New Directions Books, 1970.

Niebuhr, Reinhold. *An Interpretation of Christian Ethics*. Louisville, KY: Westminster John Knox Press, 2013.

Nouwen, Henri. *A Letter of Consolation*. New York: Harper & Row, 1982.

———. *The Return of the Prodigal Son, A Story of Homecoming*. New York: Doubleday, 1992.

Olasky, Marvin. *The Tragedy of American Compassion*. Wheaton, IL: Crossway Books, 1992.

Palmer, Parker. *Let Your Life Speak, Listening for the Voice of Vocation*. San Francisco: Jossey-Bass, 2000.

Prager, Dennis. *Happiness is a Serious Problem, A Human Nature Repair Manual*. New York: HarperCollins Publishers, 1998.

Regier, Nate, and Jeff King. *Beyond Drama, Transcending Energy Vampires*. Newton, KS: Next Element Publishing, 2013.

Rohr, Richard. *Adam's Return, The Five Promises of Male Initiation*. New York: The Crossroad Publishing Co., 2004.

———. *Falling Upward, A Spirituality of the Two Halves of Life*. San Francisco: Jossey-Bass, 2011.

Smedes, Lewis B. *Forgive and Forget, Healing the Hurts We Don't Deserve*. San Francisco: Harper Collins, 1996.

Smith, Gordon T. *Courage and Calling, Embracing Your God-Given Potential.* Downers Grove, IL: Inter-Varsity Press, 1999.ten Boom, Corrie. *The Hiding Place.* Washington, CT: Worldwide Books, 1971.

Tournier, Paul. *The Meaning of Persons.* New York: Harper & Row, 1957.

———. *The Whole Person in a Broken World.* New York: Harper & Row, 1964.

Wagner, Lynn and Dan Wagner. *Not Wasted.* Privately printed. Second edition, May 2016.

Ware, Bronnie. *The Top Five Regrets of the Dying, A Life Transformed by the Dearly Departing.* Carlsbad, CA: Hay House, Inc., 2011–12.

☐

To view the Wagner's video, "A Testimony of Forgiveness," on your smartphone, open the camera app and point it at the QR code below:

For
further exploration:

———————

Visit our Website

www.WisdomGuides.org

Made in the USA
San Bernardino, CA
17 February 2020